A TIME FOR PEACE

Biblical Meditations for Advent

A TIME FOR PEACE

Biblical Meditations for Advent

by

Rev. William F. Maestri

ALBA · HOUSE   NEW · YORK

SOCIETY OF ST. PAUL, 2187 VICTORY BLVD., STATEN ISLAND, NEW YORK 10314

Library of Congress Cataloging in Publication Data

Maestri, William.
 A time for peace.

 1. Advent—Meditations. I. Title.
BX2170.A4M3   1983   242'.33   83-22339
ISBN 0-8189-0463-1

Nihil Obstat:
John H. Miller, C.S.C.
Censor Librorum

Imprimatur:
† Philip M. Hannon
Archbishop of New Orleans
September 28, 1982

Designed, printed and bound in the United States of
America by the Fathers and Brothers of the
Society of St. Paul, 2187 Victory Boulevard,
Staten Island, New York 10314, as part of their
communications apostolate.

---

1 2 3 4 5 6 7 8 9 (Current Printing: first digit)

CONTENTS

INTRODUCTION

The whole of Sacred Scripture proclaims the following: God-is-with-us. The opening pages of Genesis tell the story of the creative love of God. The very Spirit of God is at work bringing order out of chaos. This creative, loving Spirit of God is at work in the creation of man. God's very breath of life is given to man as the one made in the Divine image and called to grow into the Divine likeness. God pronounced the work of His hands "very good." Unfortunately, man was not satisfied to be man, but sought to become like God. The Fall of humankind and its subsequent sins resulted in the alienation of the human person from the true source of life and peace. Once humankind became estranged from God it was not long before man became alienated from himself, others and the world.

However, the Bible goes on to tell us that God was not satisfied to leave His creation in this state of brokenness. The God who creates also re-creates. The God who brings all things into existence also liberates. The God who is with us is also the loving Father who is for us. Hence, after a long and patient unfolding of history, God spoke His Word into the world and our human condition. In the person of Jesus we see the very love of God made visible. Jesus is the ultimate gift and expression of God's love for us. Jesus is the final, ultimate and lasting commitment of God on our behalf. In Jesus, God says "yes" to all that is human and supportive of life.

The season of Advent is the time when we prepare for the coming of "the Word made flesh." Advent highlights the way in which we relate to time, and reveals the manner in which we wait. We can seek to conquer time by rushing headlong into the future, never pausing to reflect on where we have been or where we are going. We can try to overcome time by "killing it" in seeking one pleasure after another. We can allow time to kill our spirit by giving in to the banality and routine of the everyday. In all of these, time is our enemy which must be controlled if not conquered. We are too busy or self-important to allow the mystery of life and God to be revealed to us. The discipline of patience is too much to bear.

However, there is another way into time and this season of Advent. We learn to befriend time by being open to the mystery of God and life. We learn the discipline of patient, hopeful waiting. Such waiting is not a call to quietism or passivity. Rather, we are challenged to endure, suffer with, and hope beyond the present. In so doing, we redeem the present and offer it up to God in an act of gratitude. We are no longer ruled by the tyranny of the clock. We are liberated by the mystery of the present and of God working in our lives. Advent is the call to join God when, "in the fullness of time," He became one like us out of love.

This book of biblical meditations is offered with the hope that the general reader and the preacher will befriend time and the mystery of God during this Advent season. The plan of the book is simple. The Scripture readings for the weekdays of Advent are summarized along with a meditation. There is also a piece on the Immaculate Conception and a closing reflection on the birth of Jesus. Hopefully this will help the preacher in preparing daily homilies for the season of Advent. The general reader can benefit by using this book as a resource for daily meditation and the reading of Scripture.

I would like to express my gratitude to Paul Hart and Connie Schwander for cheerfully typing the entire manuscript. This book is dedicated to the students of Mercy Academy and the seminarians of St. Joseph Seminary. They have taught me much about the need for patient waiting and the mystery of growth through God's grace. Finally, my sincere thanks is expressed to the Society of St. Paul, Alba House, and Father Timothy for allowing me to offer these biblical meditations on Advent.

> *William F. Maestri*
> *St. Joseph Seminary*
> *St. Benedict, La.*

We know then that in our own existence and in the destiny of mankind, whether by life or death, we fall into the hands of the God whom we must leave nameless and of whom it can nevertheless be said that for us He is eternal light, eternal life, ineffable glory, peace without end, since He has enabled us to forget ourselves and to be for Him.

> *Karl Rahner, S.J.*

A TIME FOR PEACE

Biblical Meditations for Advent

Monday of the First Week

Isaiah 2:1-5

Yahweh is the Lord of history and the loving creator of all that exists. Yahweh calls a people, Israel, to be His instrument of salvation to all peoples. Yahweh desires that all come to know Him and be part of His saving covenant. Isaiah presents a vision of hope for all humankind. Yahweh will gather all the nations to live in justice and peace. The foundation of this unity is obedience to the will of God. There will be no need for nations to train for war. Yahweh's peace will be established.

Isaiah 4:2-6 (Year A)

The glory and power of Yahweh is made known through the fidelity of His people. All who remain faithful to the Lord will receive a blessing. What is required is a turning from idol worship and from lack of compassion for the poor. Yahweh is a God who hears the cry of the oppressed and responds to their needs.

Matthew 8:5-11

The themes of salvation and healing are present in our Gospel reading. Jesus responds to the faith of the centurion by healing his servant. This miracle indicates that Jesus comes to announce God's saving, healing presence for all people. Both

Jew and Gentile are called to be part of the new covenant. God's saving will is universal and cannot be limited to a specific group. What is required is the unconditional faith shown by the centurion.

PEACE

At one time or another, all of us have longed for Alladin's magic lamp and the three wishes. For the more religious among us, we would like to trade places with Solomon and have one wish granted by Yahweh. What would we desire? Money? Power? Fame? Popularity? Maybe we would be like Solomon and choose wisdom. If we read the newspaper and watch the television news, maybe we would desire peace. Certainly, during the season of Advent our thoughts turn to peace. We want peace to find its way into our heart, and quiet the fears and anxieties that so often grip us. We desire peace for our family and those we love. Peace is the libation that heals the broken relationships that mean so much to us. Along with the prophet Isaiah, we want peace to come to the human family. We desire the day when all nations "shall beat their swords into plowshares and their spears into pruning hooks." Yes, peace would certainly be high on the contemporary list of gifts we need.

We need to ask just what is peace? How do we go about obtaining peace? Let us first indicate that peace is *not* quietism or merely being left alone. To be at peace is not to be ignored. Rather, peace is essentially God's gift. In the words of St. Augustine: "peace, that magnificent gift from God, even understood as one of the fleeting things of earth, no sweeter word is heard, no more desirable wish is longed for and no better discovery can be made than this gift." The gift of peace is grounded in God's loving, just will for all people. The prophet Isaiah reminds us that peace comes from walking in the way of the Lord. Peace comes to the individual and the nation that are willing to be instructed by Him.

Isaiah goes on to indicate (Is 4:2-6, the Year A reading) that there can be no peace where justice and concern for the poor are forgotten. The covenant of Yahweh which offers peace demands justice. Peace is the gift of God to those individuals and communities that seek the common good. Justice requires that we respect the dignity of all persons and love one another as brothers and sisters who have the same loving Father, redeeming Brother and sustaining Spirit. The civil authorities are given a special opportunity to serve the cause of justice and hence promote peace. All institutions and social structures which unfairly discriminate and dehumanize must be transformed into structures which enhance the sacredness of human life.

While peace is God's gift, we are called to take active responsibility for seeing that the gift is accepted and applied. Simply put: peace is God's gift entrusted to each of us. We are called to extend God's peace and healing to all those corners of the world we touch each day. We do this in various ways. We respect life in all its forms, and give praise to God as the Lord of Life. We work for a just society in which the cries of the poor and powerless never reach the ears of Yahweh because we have heard them and responded. To the best of our abilities, we study and become informed about justice-peace issues and how they relate to the Gospel and the social teachings of the Church. We take the responsibility of peace seriously when we elect leaders who are sensitive to the needs of all people. In the words of Pope John Paul II: "The Church supports and encourages all serious efforts for peace. It unhesitatingly proclaims that the activity of all those who devote the best of their energies to peace forms part of God's plan for salvation in Jesus Christ."

Advent is the season of "peace on earth and glad tidings to all people of good will." The peace of Christ is also meant for our hearts. God spoke His ultimate Word into our world to bring salvation and healing to all who believe. The centurion went on his way confident that Jesus heals. Advent is the season which reminds us of God's love. Jesus comes to heal us from sin and remove all that keeps us from God. Let us pray for the faith and courage to accept this healing. In so doing, we will know the peace of the One who is our true peace.

Tuesday of the First Week

Isaiah
11:1-10

The prophet Isaiah speaks of the time when Yahweh will raise up a king to rule the people in justice, peace and obedience to the Lord's will. Such a ruler will have the very spirit of Yahweh resting within him. The characteristics of a ruler pleasing to God are listed: wisdom, understanding, counsel, strength, knowledge, fortitude and fear of the Lord. Through this ruler the task of reconciliation will be realized. There will be no more poor among the people. Nature will be tamed of its wildness. The Israelites will be a light to the Gentiles and a source of hope. Ultimately the whole creation will be filled with the knowledge of God.

Luke
10:21-24

One of the major themes in St. Luke's Gospel is that of joy. In this selection, Luke tells us that Jesus rejoices in the Holy Spirit and offers prayers of praise to the Father. The great mysteries of the Kingdom, the gift of Jesus, and salvation are offered to all who have faith. One comes to know God as Father through faith in Jesus. Jesus comes to tell us that God is our gracious Father.

OUR GRACIOUS GOD

One of the first lessons we learn is that of competition and the need to win. We compete for the attention of our parents and teachers. We compete for jobs in the economic marketplace. We even compete for the girl or guy of our dreams. The law of competition is especially pronounced in the American context. Blue ribbons, gold stars and trophies are the acceptance-symbols of our early identity. Later, it is the big house, big paycheck and summer home that prove to others and ourselves that we have made it. We are OK! Unfortunately, such competition can easily lead us to view others as adversaries and even enemies. Each day becomes a new series of challenges which threaten our self-worth. Each new person we meet becomes a potential competitor trying to get the esteem and approval of others. Equally unfortunate is the concept of God that flows from this competitive orientation. God is a demanding judge who is in constant need of proof that we love Him. We need to constantly live up to the rigorous demands of this God who only loves and accepts winners.

The Gospel of St. Luke offers us another way. Luke invites us to live, not by competition, but through graciousness. To live through graciousness is to experience life as a gift. Each day is an opportunity to grow closer to others and live in communion with our brothers and sisters. Above all, to live in graciousness is to be open to God as our loving Father. When we live in graciousness, we do not need to compete, grasp or conquer anyone or anything. Life is not a series of challenges which affirm or deny our self-worth. Rather, life is a precious gift that we are called to accept and share. Above all, living in graciousness offers us a clue about the very nature of God.

Jesus prays in the joy of the Holy Spirit out of thanksgiving for the gracious will of the Father. The Father has given and made known everything to Jesus. Jesus came to make the graciousness of God's love known. However, it is hidden from the worldly-wise and business-smart. The mysteries of the Kingdom and Jesus are hidden from those who are blinded by their own achievements and trophies. Those who live by competition approach Jesus with a whole series of accomplishments in order to win acceptance. Yet Jesus is not concerned about what we have or produce. Jesus is interested in each of us. It is the quality of our heart that is of ultimate concern. Even the prophets and kings do not experience what the disciples see and hear. In the final analysis it is to "the merest children," who come to Jesus in faith, that the Kingdom is revealed.

Advent is the season which reminds us of the depth of God's love. Jesus is God's loving Word for each of us. Furthermore, we are called to love one another. To live in God's gracious presence liberates us from the compulsion to compete with others. Through the Spirit of Jesus, we come to experience others as gifts from God. We come to see our common humanity grounded in the Father's love. Then we too can rejoice in the Holy Spirit.

Wednesday of the First Week

Isaiah
25:6-10

The prophet Isaiah paints a magnificent vision of the day in which God's Kingdom will be fully realized. All the peoples of the world will be united into one family. The divisions of humankind will give way to that time when all veils are destroyed. In God's Kingdom there will be no one who is lacking. There will be no pain, suffering, sin or death. God not only creates but also saves and heals. Isaiah ends on a note of joy and exaltation. No one who turns to Yahweh will be disappointed.

Matthew
15:29-37

The vision of Isaiah, which presents God as the one who heals and saves, is continued in our Gospel. Jesus, the compassion of God, heals those who are broken in body and spirit. Jesus is constantly sensitive to the needs of those whom he serves. Moved with pity, Jesus feeds the hungry crowd. This is a reminder of the Eucharist which will be given for eternal life. Also, one should note the abundant generosity of Jesus—"When they gathered up the fragments left over, these filled seven hampers."

GOD-FOR-US

Among the more important characteristics of a true friend is that of simply being-for-us. The true friend is one who does not judge us, but accepts us for who we are. The true friend challenges us to be the best we can be. When we are hurt by life and bruised by "the slings and arrows of outrageous fortune," we need someone to be for us. We come to value the presence of the other who allows us to become part of their concerns. The person and friend who is for us says, "I am not sure I can say or do the right thing but I am sure I will be with you and for you." It is through such experiences and with such friends that we realize the power of another's presence.

In our first reading from the prophet Isaiah, the people cry out to the Lord for salvation and deliverance. The Lord responds in a way that far exceeds any human expectation. The generosity of God evokes from the people a joyous cry: "Behold our God, to whom we looked to save us! . . . he saved us!" Isaiah uses a wealth of images to present the abundant kindness of God. The mountains of the Lord will gather all peoples. There will be no poverty or lack of good things. Yahweh assembles the nations to an endless banquet. The Lord wipes away all pain, suffering, tears and death. Above all, the Lord removes their sin and calls the nations to live in justice and peace.

The fullness of God's saving presence is found in Jesus. God's solidarity with the human condition becomes visible in the Word made flesh. Our God is one who is concerned about human needs and responds out of love. Matthew tells us that large numbers seek Jesus out in order to be healed. The good news of God that Jesus announces is one of healing and wholeness. The crippled and deformed are made strong. The mute are free to praise God. The blind see in Jesus God's very love for all people. Jesus is moved to compassion by the many needs of those who come in faith. The large crowd which followed Jesus is hungry and there are so few resources handy. However, he will provide and be for the people. Jesus takes the loaves and fish, gives thanks, and distributes them to the crowd. Not only are all full, but there is a surplus. The compassion of God revealed in Jesus is much more than we could ever hope for. God supplies our every need and more.

Advent is the time in which we come to experience just how much God is for us. Each of us in our own way is in need of God's compassion and healing presence. What are the ways in which we are blind, lame, deformed and in the grip of sin? The vision of Isaiah and the gift of Jesus are especially for us. For our readings are not simply a recounting of what God and Jesus did once, long ago. Our readings are a constant reminder of what God continues to do for us each day. The mountain of the Lord in Isaiah and the mountainside by the Sea of Galilee have been transformed into the Eucharistic table of the Lord. Each time we gather in his name, we remember just how much God loves us in Jesus. We celebrate our solidarity with each other, and long for that day when the entire human family will be one. We eat the Lord's Supper and are satisfied with the bread of eternal life. We too look to the Lord for salvation. Let us rejoice and be glad, for He has come among us and saved us!

Thursday of the First Week

Isaiah 26:1-6   The Old Testament tells the story of the old covenant relationship between Yahweh and the people of Israel. Yahweh is their God who cares for them and gets involved in their history. Israel is called to be faithful to the covenant relationship. There is to be no idol worship, and justice is to flow like a mighty stream. If the people of Israel are like this, they will know peace. If not, Israel suffers the consequences. Isaiah is calling the people to be faithful to the covenant. They must be a nation which loves justice so as to enjoy peace. The Lord is a just God who "humbles those in high places, and the lofty city he brings down." Yahweh is not indifferent to the poor. Israel cannot be, either.

Matthew 8:24-27

Throughout our readings from the prophet Isaiah, we see how much God wants all people to be saved. Everyone is called to worship on God's holy mountain. However, Jesus reminds the disciples that it is never enough to merely render lip service or proclaim bold words. Ultimately one must be moved to action on behalf of the Kingdom. Faith in Jesus must find expression in both our words and deeds. First we must hear the word and understand it. But then we must put the Gospel into practice.

DOERS OF THE WORD

We Americans are a pragmatic lot. That is, our primary question is "does it work?" We like the practical and the "hard-headed." We have little patience with theory and ideas. In the final analysis, our views must have "cash value" in the everyday world. Above all, we want results and we prize deeds over words. The American hero is a man who is strong and silent. The man of few words is the one who can be counted on when the going gets tough. Actions speak louder than words. In fact, we are often suspicious of the person who talks too much. We wonder what he is trying to hide.

In our readings today, both Isaiah and Jesus place a high premium on action. The prophet Isaiah reminds the Israelites that they are like no other people. They belong to Yahweh. They are His through the covenant, and Yahweh is theirs. Yahweh does not merely say that He loves the Israelites. He shows them through His mighty deeds in history. The most important of these deeds are the Exodus and the settlement of the Promised Land. Yahweh's care and love is *active* and dynamic. God does not stay isolated in the heavens, but enters into the concerns of His people. Yahweh expects the people of Israel to be active in their response to Him. They do this through obedience to God's will and in the seeking after justice. It is not enough for Israel to be God's people in name only. Israel must *do* God's will by loving Him alone and by taking care of community members. Throughout the Old Testament, the prophets will continually remind Israel of her covenant responsibilities. Israel must be "a nation that is just, one that keeps faith." It must "trust in the Lord forever!"

Jesus says to his disciples, the ones chosen by him, that they must both hear the word and act on it. Just because one walks with Jesus and witnesses the miracles, there is no assurance of salvation. If one remains just a hearer of the word, the Gospel is mere sentiment or dry intellectual information. If, on the other hand, one puts the Gospel into practice, it grows and develops. One is able to pay the cost of discipleship. The good news of Jesus becomes just that—good news—and we must share it with others. No doubt, many came to Jesus seeking all sorts of things. Unfortunately, many go away sad once they hear what is required. The true disciple is one who *does* the will of the Father.

Advent is the season in which we wait and celebrate the active, loving involvement of God in our lives. The coming of Jesus is the revelation of just how much God cares for us. Jesus is the ultimate affirmation of all that is human. Jesus is God's irreversible "yes" to our history. During this season, we prepare for the birth of Jesus. However, this preparation is never passive. We must be like the wise man in our Gospel who puts God's word into action and builds a house on rock. Advent is the opportune time to grow in love of the Eucharist, to pray the Scriptures, and to be of service to others in need. During Advent, we are not to be loud seekers of the spectacular. Rather, in patient hope we try each day to do the will of our Father. In so doing, the words of the responsorial Psalm will be ours: "Blessed is the one who comes in the name of the Lord."

Friday of the First Week

Isaiah
29:17-24

The prophet Isaiah has been reminding the people of their sinfulness. Israel has played "fast and loose" with the covenant. Idolatry and injustice have been rampant. Hence, Yahweh's peace is not to be found in the land. However, the prophet also speaks words of comfort, encouragement and hope. Even though Israel is unfaithful, Yahweh will never abandon the covenant. Isaiah says it will be "a very little while," and then the healing of Yahweh will occur. Lebanon will be an orchard. The deaf will hear. The blind will see. The lowly and the poor will rejoice in the Lord. Those who continue to reject the Lord will be cut off and left to their evil. However, Isaiah's message is hopeful: "Those who err in spirit shall acquire understanding."

Matthew
9:27-31

Jesus comes to announce the Kingdom of God. With the coming Kingdom there is healing and liberation from all that enslaves people to sin. Jesus, the true Light of Life, is requested by two blind men to cure them. Jesus asks if they believe he can do this. After they profess their faith, Jesus cures them and cautions against making the cure public. However, these two men go off proclaiming Jesus throughout the region.

THE GUIDING LIGHT

Making our way through Advent is also making our way through the commercialization of "the season to be jolly." From the day after Thanksgiving right up to Christmas itself, we are pressured to buy and give. Naturally, we must also make a list and check it twice for all the things we want. Without throwing a damper on this buying mania, let us ask a different question: what is the one gift we possess that money can't buy? Of the many gifts of life, to name one you most prize? A hard question. Among the many answers that one could offer, certainly the gift of sight must rank high. It is through the gift of sight that we can thrill to stars on a winter's night; the smile of a child; and the setting of the sun at day's end. Sight is a gift few of us would part with.

The Scriptures speak of sight, but in a deeper way. Sight

is not only the ability to see with the eye, but more importantly with the heart. Sight is the ability to see God's saving presence in one's life and in the history of the community. The prophet Isaiah in our first reading says, "the eyes of the blind shall see." Israel has been blind to the requirements of the covenant. She has lost sight of what is required of Yahweh's people. Idolatry and injustice are holding sway over the people. Repentance and conversion are required. The prophets are sent by Yahweh to call the people back to the Lord. Israel has lost her way and ventured deeper into the valley of darkness. Isaiah comes with a message of hope. Very soon the day of deliverance will arrive. Out of the gloom and darkness of the present moment, a light will shine and the eyes of the blind shall see.

The true Light that gives Life has come in the person of Jesus. Although the two men in our Gospel reading are physically blind, they possess some level of spiritual insight into the person of Jesus. These two men recognize Jesus as the compassion of God, and request him to heal them out of pity (compassion). Jesus does not immediately respond to their request, but tests their faith. He wants to hear from them that they possess confidence and faith in his ability to let them see. Jesus restores their sight by touching their eyes. He does not respond to the needs of others in a distant way. The healing ministry of Jesus always touches the person in need. The Incarnation is the love of God made flesh, and the healing ministry of Jesus continues the incarnation of God's love. The blind now see, and go about giving praise to God. We often go about blind to the miracle of God's love in our lives and our everyday world. It is so easy for us to be overcome by the banalities, profaneness and sinfulness of our world. Yet also present is the redeeming, healing love of God. We can only see and experience God's love through a confident faith in the person of Jesus. The request of the two men in our Gospel is the ongoing request of the Christian life: Jesus, help us to see with the eyes of faith. Jesus, help us to see and experience your loving, redeeming presence in our world and our hearts. In response Jesus asks, "Are you confident I can do this?" The two men in our Gospel answered, "Yes, Lord." Let us make their answer ours as well.

Saturday of the First Week

Isaiah
30:19-21,
23-26

The image of the prophet is often one of judgment and anger. The prophet goes about proclaiming doom and gloom. To be sure, sin is offensive to God, and the prophet clearly indicates what will happen if people persist in rejecting God and the covenant. However, there is another side to the prophet and his message. Isaiah announces an end to weeping and a time in which the Lord will supply every need. In fact, the Lord will reveal himself to the people so they will not lose their way. The abundant love of God will be evidenced in the fruitfulness of nature. In one of the most thrilling verses in Scripture, Isaiah proclaims, "the Lord binds up the wounds of his people, he will heal the bruises left by his blows." Punishment for sin is real, but greater in abundance is the healing love of Yahweh.

Matthew
9:35-
10:1, 6-8

St. Matthew paints a powerful picture of Jesus. Jesus goes about teaching and acting on behalf of the people. He proclaims

the good news of the reign of God. The
good news is connected with the ministry
of healing. Jesus, the Good Shepherd, is
moved to pity at the needs of the people.
There are many needs, and so there must
be many who go forth announcing the
Good News and ministering to the sick and
possessed.

TRUE GIVING

Ralph Waldo Emerson once said, "The only true and
lasting gift is the gift of oneself." Emerson was reminding us
that if giving is to be more than a formality, it must involve
us in some way. If our giving is not to be a means to control
others, we must offer ourselves out of love and freedom.
Perhaps this is why so little true giving takes place. There is
an awful risk involved. To offer oneself to the other is to be
vulnerable to rejection and pain. It is one thing to reject a
gift that cost dollars and cents, but it is quite another to reject
the giver. Hence, we can seek safety behind our presents
without a real personal involvement. We learn this lesson
early in life. The teacher assigns the class the task of making
a Christmas card for one's parents. It may take the child
weeks to design. The big day arrives and the card is given.
Naturally much more is involved. The child is returning the
love of his parents in a profound act of self-giving. The
child, filled with anticipation and love, is making Emerson's
true and lasting gift. We can only hope the parent's response
is worthy of the gift.

Both of our readings from Scripture speak to us of true
giving. God, through the Exodus and covenant, gave Himself to Israel. Yahweh was not satisfied to remain in the
heavens in some form of regal splendor. The Exodus and

the covenant are a perpetual reminder that Yahweh *cares* and is involved with His people. Yahweh is like no other God. He reveals Himself and gives Himself to Israel. It is little wonder that the prophets often use the symbol of marriage to express the relationship between Yahweh and Israel. The covenant requires a total gift of self. Isaiah reminds Israel just how gracious and giving is the Lord. The Lord gives bread, water, rain, an abundant harvest and many animals so that Israel's weeping will be no more. Above all, Yahweh gives Himself so the people can see with their own eyes and hear the voice of the Lord. Yahweh's self-gift will heal their bruises and bind up their wounds.

The fullness of God's self-giving is revealed in Jesus. Jesus is the good news of God's reign. The sick are cured and those in the grip of Satan are liberated. The message of Jesus is most profound: "The reign of God is at hand!" In other words, the active sovereign presence of God is at work in Jesus in an ultimate way. The rule of God is present in Jesus. The hope of Israel is about to be fulfilled in him. Salvation comes to Israel and then the whole world through the preaching of Jesus and his disciples. He comes to announce that God is loving compassion. Jesus reveals just how much the heart of God is moved.

Our Gospel reading ends with Jesus telling the disciples that the gifts of the Kingdom and the Good News must be shared. They have received much, and much is expected of them. The disciples have been given the mysteries of the Kingdom, and in gratitude they must give to others. So it is with us. Through baptism, we have been made a new creation. The Christian vocation is a call to labor on behalf of the Kingdom, and through our words and deeds to help advance the compassionate reign of God. We cannot allow the gift of our faith in Jesus to become a private possession. The gift we have received, we are to give as a gift.

The seasons of Advent and Christmas are times when we are busy giving and receiving. Yet so much of it is empty and meaningless. There is often little of ourself in our gifts. The birth of Jesus reminds us of the depth of God's self-giving. What's more, we are challenged to continue the story. We are to give as we have received. The reign of God is at hand!

Monday of the Second Week

Isaiah
35:1-10

The most profound experience in Israel's history is the Exodus. Yahweh cares for His people and acts to save them. He is the Lord of history and life. Not only does Yahweh liberate, He also leads Israel into a land of abundance. Unfortunately, Israel is not always faithful and responsive. Idolatry and injustice are constant temptations. Also, the Israelites want to be like the other nations. They want a king and be able to enter into political alliances. The prophets continually remind the people of Israel that they are not like other nations. Yahweh is their strength and hope. Isaiah offers an impressive vision of the Messianic Age. It is one of abundance, life, growth, healing, and above all peace. The Messiah will bring about a time of universal reconciliation and prosperity. Those who have gone astray will be brought to the Lord's mountain and sing His praises.

Luke
5:17-26

One of the major themes of St. Luke's Gospel is Jesus' power to forgive sins. Also evident is the Lucan theme of joy and the need to praise God. Jesus is brought a paralytic on a mat. Seeing the faith of the crowd, Jesus forgives the man's sins. However, the Pharisees accuse Jesus of blasphemy. Only God can forgive sins. However, Jesus responds by healing the man of his moral and physical infirmity. The man is liberated from sin and its power to keep one in bondage. But Jesus also heals the man of his physical paralysis. The man goes home praising God, and the crowd is filled with awe.

HEAL ME—BUT NOT YET

St. Augustine, in his spiritual autobiography, *The Confessions*, prayed to be made pure and chaste but he quickly added that God could wait awhile. The pleasures of the flesh had to be brought under control, but Augustine was in no hurry for the conversion. The same delaying tactic is often used when it comes to sickness. We learn early in life that being sick has its benefits. We are excused from all our responsibilities. We need not go to school or work when we are sick. People don't expect too much of us. Life can be lived in the "comfort" lane. Also, being sick turns us into an object of pity and attention by family and authority figures alike. Being sick brings us into the spotlight and we receive a surplus of tender, loving care. Finally, sickness can be used to excuse our bad manners and moods. Hence we might be tempted to alter Augustine's dictum into: heal me—but not yet!

Whenever Israel violates the covenant, she suffers the consequences. She disobeys Yahweh and is taken into exile. The people experience themselves as barren, sterile, feeble, frightened, blind, deaf and filled with gloom. Poor Israel! How could this happen? How could Yahweh allow this to take place to His beloved? But Isaiah tells the people they can't engage in such self-pity. Yahweh will usher in the Messianic Age and bring about a time of healing, restoration and reconciliation. Yahweh will ransom His people and return them to Zion. Israel is not excused from the covenant even in exile. During the time of healing, Israel is called to follow the Lord in a state of joy and gladness.

In our Gospel reading, Jesus heals the paralytic. St. Luke tells us that the man, once cured, goes home praising God. The crowd is filled with awe and gives praise to God. The Pharisees are upset and accuse Jesus of blasphemy. After healing the man of his physical infirmity and forgiving his sins, Jesus says, "Return to your house." This man could not return home in the same way he had done for so many years. He was now cured. He was liberated from his moral and physical defects. He must now begin to live in a new way. He could no longer rely on others, make excuses, and avoid everyday responsibilities. The man who knew only a mat now stood erect and went home praising God. The rest of this man's story we don't know. We can only hope he continued to walk erect and praise God.

Advent is a time of healing and forgiveness. We are called to examine all those dark and broken areas of our life. We need to look at the ways in which we have traveled to a distant land away from the Lord's mountain. This is never easy. Not only must we change, but we must accept our healing. This means we can't hold on to the past and make excuses. We are healed and cannot give in to fear. We are to be strong. Through Jesus our sins are forgiven, and we go boldly into the future proclaiming what God has done for us. The temptation is to remain in exile and self-pity. Who wants to get off a mat and have their sins forgiven? That's too demanding and complex. Self-pity, and blaming the devil are much easier. Yahweh and Jesus will have none of it.

The Israelites must return to Zion singing a new song. The man must get off the mat and live in a new way. So it is with us. We too must sing a new song and live a new life. In so doing, incredible things continue to happen!

Tuesday of the Second Week

Isaiah
40:1-11

Israel is in exile because she trusted in a political alliance rather than the covenant. Israel's strength has never been in chariots and charioteers. On the contrary, military power has always been used to oppress and enslave Israel. Israel has been taken far beyond Jerusalem and is in exile in Babylon. In the midst of their guilt, confusion, anger and despair the words of Deutero-Isaiah are proclaimed: "Comfort, give comfort to my people says your God. Speak tenderly to Jerusalem, and proclaim to her that her service is at an end, her guilt is removed." Israel has received a just punishment for her infidelity. But the love and tenderness of Yahweh is more abundant. Yahweh will restore Israel so that she will be a sign to the nations of hope and salvation. Yahweh is the true and good Shepherd who gathers His flock and feeds them with care.

Matthew
18:12-14

These three brief verses contain one of the most precious insights into the nature of God and the mission of Jesus. God desires that all people respond to His love and be saved. Unfortunately, sin has entered the

world and humankind has gone astray.
But Yahweh would not leave us alone in
our sin. He establishes a covenant and
sends the prophets to speak tenderly to
Israel and all the nations. Finally, the
depth of God's love is made visible in His
only Son, Jesus. The sending of the Word
is God's call to all who wandered away.
The Word leaves the Father in order to
search out the lost ones—and heaven
rejoices!

LOST AND FOUND

One of the most traumatic experiences of a young child
is to get lost in a crowd. I can still remember going to a large
department store with my mother. While looking at all the
wonderful things, I lost touch of my mother's hand. I
panicked. I began to run about looking for my mother, but
only succeeded in becoming more lost. The panic grew until
I began to cry. I still remember a nice lady coming to my
rescue. She told me everything would be alright. She would
help me find my mother. She took my hand in a firm but
gentle way. Before we reached our destination, I spotted my
mother. I bolted to her. After a few moments, I turned to see
the lady who helped me. She was gone. But her kindness
remains with me to this day. The unknown lady helped a
little boy who was lost. I am sure God has not forgotten her
kindness to one who went astray.

I recount this story because it personalized for me the
story of Israel and the one lost sheep. Israel has become
dazzled by the power of her neighbors. She too wants to be
like them. Yet Israel is called to be special through its relationship with Yahweh. Yahweh respects freedom, and so

Israel must suffer the consequences and experience exile. In a far-away land Israel is lost, in a state of panic, and surrounded by unfamiliar and unfriendly faces. The words of this unknown prophet (Deutero-Isaiah) come to Israel. They are words of comfort, tenderness, freedom, abundance and peace. Yahweh is like a shepherd who loves, cares for and feeds his flock. He will not rest until all are safe.

The comfort and tenderness of God are fully revealed with the coming of Jesus. Through the birth of Jesus, the lasting forgiveness of sins and subsequent peace are established. The glory of God is revealed as suffering, forgiving love. Jesus is the true and good shepherd who comes to call all people to reconciliation and life. Most especially, Jesus comes to announce the good news of forgiveness to those who have turned away from God. God's desire to save everyone is so abundant that all the limits of human understanding are broken. Jesus comes to search for the sinner who has become too much one with the world.

Two additional points in our Gospel reading are worthy of reflection. There is no guarantee that the search will be successful. Not even the greatness of God's love can cancel out human freedom and responsibility. Jesus says, "*If* he succeeds in finding it . . ." However, God does not want anyone to be lost. Our second point is the joy which fills God over repentance. Our God is not a God of punishment but one of life. Jesus is sent to bring us life to the full.

Advent is the season of healing and being found. Jesus is the loving Word sent by the Father to bring us life and peace. God is not searching for us in order to recount our sins and make us dwell on the past. Rather, Jesus comes to announce comfort and to speak tenderly to our hearts. Our sins are forgiven and our guilt is removed. We celebrate the birth of Jesus and the hope of new life. We are called to quiet our frantic search for happiness. In faith and childlike trust we are to open our hearts to Jesus, who leads us with joy to the Father. Being lost is no fun. Take it from a little boy who long ago experienced the happiness of being found.

Wednesday of the Second Week

Isaiah
40:25-31

The reading from Isaiah speaks directly to the exiled condition of Israel. Israel is faint, weary and without hope. She has placed her trust in false gods and in political alliances, and has allowed injustice to spread in the land. In effect, the covenant has been ignored. Isaiah reminds the people of the greatness of the Lord. Yahweh has created everything that exists. His power and majesty are evidenced in creation. Israel cannot say she is ignorant of the Lord's will. For who else has Yahweh revealed Himself? Above all, the prophet reminds the people that the Lord is the Holy One. In fact Yahweh is the essence of holiness, and wants a people who are holy as well.

Matthew
11:28-30

The care and love of Jesus for the people is contrasted with the self-serving concerns of the Pharisees. The Pharisees desire their own glory, and use their position for their own advantage. They have no concern for the people or the will of God. The Pharisees use religion to keep people in line and to hold onto their own power. By contrast, Jesus comes to proclaim the good

news of salvation. To the weary, the faint
of heart and the lonely, Jesus announces
the year of the Lord's favor. Jesus is not
interested in his own glory, but comes to
do the Father's will. He is "the man for
others" who comes to speak a word of
comfort to the weary and to those bruised
by life.

THE LIGHT BURDEN

The pace of contemporary life often leaves us more
driven than driving. Everyday life seems to have a pace and
a logic (or better, illogic) all its own. Schedules, events and
deadlines have us in their life-consuming grip. Life has
always had its demands and frustrations. In less technologi-
cal and less rationally constructed societies, most of the
burdens were associated with the physical demands of stay-
ing alive. One needed to gather food, find shelters and keep
warm. However, today for much of the world this is no
longer true. (Naturally, too much of the world continues to
live in conditions that are sub-human and which demand a
response from the rich nations.) The burdens of today are
more internal, and affect the soul and mind. Psychiatrists
are telling us that more and more of their patients are
complaining of meaninglessness. There seems to be such
little fulfillment in life even after one has gained the whole
world. More people are coming to realize that the bread and
trophies of this world will not sustain the human spirit. The
human person has a spiritual dimension that must be
nourished. We realize that no surplus of material posses-
sions can bring us the peace we all search for and need.
People all over the world are once again on the march
searching for "the things that really matter."

In our first reading, the search for true peace and prosperity has been part of Israel's long history. From the Exodus to the Exile and the Restoration, Israel has been less than faithful to Yahweh. Perhaps the covenant should be cancelled for the establishment of a monarchy. Maybe Israel should be like the other nations, and seek protection in military strength and political alliances. Yet after all these side adventures, Israel must return to the Lord for true consolation. It is Yahweh who gives strength to the weary and envigorates those grown tired. Simply put, Yahweh does not only establish the covenant. He also sustains the people in remaining faithful. Those who hope in the Lord will find that they have strength for the journey and will not be disappointed.

Our Gospel reading must be included among the most moving passages in Scripture. Jesus, the gentle and humble Son of the Father, comes to refresh all who are burdened by life. He comes to give rest to the weary and to lift the burdens of sin and guilt. The Pharisees had turned the covenant into a heavy yoke which cut deep into one's spirit. They had perverted the covenant into a religion which did not give life. Religion became one more burden of an already lifeless existence. The Romans made everyday life an insult. The Pharisees turned the hope and consolation of Israel into a legalistic system of control.

Jesus is saying that he comes as the true hope and peace of all humankind. He comes to proclaim the Good News. The bondage of sin, guilt and death do not have the final word in our lives or in human history. God's love poured forth in Jesus will be ultimately victorious. We need not run madly chasing the trophies of this world. Jesus is our true peace and refreshment. In the midst of our weary and burdensome life, the words of Jesus come to us: "My yoke is easy and my burden light." Along with St. Paul, let us "put on Christ" so that we will "run and not grow weary, walk and not grow faint."

Thursday of the Second Week

Isaiah
41:13-20

The prophet reaches deep into Israel's past and recalls the greatest of Yahweh's mighty deeds—the Exodus from Egypt. Yahweh grasped Israel by the hand and brought her from slavery to freedom; from oppression to a land flowing with all good things. Israel knew the Lord to be her Liberator, Savior and Sustainer. Unfortunately, Israel has forgotten the Exodus and the Sinai covenant. Idolatry and injustice have become part of everyday life. Hence Israel has fallen on hard times and is now in exile. But all is not lost. Yahweh will once again respond to Israel's cries for deliverance. Once again Israel will be a great nation, and remain so, if only she obeys Yahweh. She must not rejoice in the glories of this world, which disappoint and quickly fade. Rather, it is in the Holy One of Israel that the people know joy and peace. Anyone who is in need will be satisfied. The Lord will bring forth water in the desert; the wasteland will be fruitful; and the needy will be so no longer. Yahweh will do all of this so that everyone will know how faithful and powerful is the Holy One.

Matthew
11:11-15

Jesus offers us a clear insight into the dangers of being a prophet and proclaiming the Kingdom of God. Violence has often been the response of those who either resist the reign of God or who want to use it for their own selfish ends. The Pharisees see the Kingdom as a challenge to their own power and control. The Zealots want to use the Kingdom to expel the Romans and be politically independent. However, the Kingdom proclaimed by Moses, Elijah, Ezekiel, and now the Baptist is a call to change. Jesus is the Kingdom, and if one is to know him as the Christ one must be converted in the heart. John the Baptist is the greatest man born of a woman, because it is his burden and glory to prepare the way of the Lord. It is John who comes to point out the Lamb who removes sins. John's vocation is to grow less so that Jesus can grow more.

THE GREATEST

How do we measure greatness? Is it found in power, fame, fortune or the outstanding achievements of men and women who selflessly work on behalf of others? Perhaps greatness is a combination of all these in various measures. We are all familiar with the boxer who went about proclaiming, "I am the greatest!" Many were turned off by this self-glorification. It seems that greatness is a recognition bestowed by others rather than a self-acknowledgment. It is not enough to be great—one must be humble as well. Greatness is not something we seek, but it seems to seek us out.

Often, it pays a call on the most unsuspecting of us. We build statues to those whom we call great. However, we just don't like them posing for the statue too quickly!

Israel was called to be a "great nation" from the time of Abraham. She would be Yahweh's instrument for the salvation of the whole world. From Israel would arise the Messiah to usher in the age of justice, peace and prosperity. Israel was to be a great nation because of what the Lord was to do through her. Her greatness was a gift from Yahweh, who chose her to be His own. Israel, for her part, was to remain faithful to the covenant. At every turn in Israel's history, Yahweh was there for her. Yahweh formed, liberated and sustained His people. The greatness of Israel was her relationship with Yahweh as the God who cares and is involved in her history. This covenant relationship established Israel as a new, double-edged sword. The Lord's judgment and salvation would come through her.

Not only did Yahweh select a nation to take an active part in salvation, but He raised up individuals as well. The prophets came to announce God's word and call the people to prepare themselves for His coming. In our Gospel reading, Jesus calls John the Baptizer the greatest man born of woman. Why is this so? John is nothing but an itinerant preacher who travels about calling people to change and give up sin. People must prepare for the Lord. He dresses funny and has a strange diet (perhaps a health-food freak?). So we ask again: why is John so great? Simply put: John is absolutely faithful to his mission in the plan of salvation. Like Mary, John sees his work within a larger reality. He knows that he is to grow less so that Jesus can become more visible and lasting. The greatness of John is his ability to let go once his work is done. He must hand over disciples and all the groundwork to the "Lamb who takes away the sins of the world."

Let us not stop with the tribute by Jesus to John; there is much more. Jesus goes on to say, "Yet the least born into the kingdom of God is greater than he." These words are for us. Through our baptism we are born into the Kingdom of God, and are called to do the great works of God each day. We are to walk wet in our baptismal waters until we attain the full measure of Jesus living in us. Yet, in many ways we continue the work of John the Baptist. In our ordinary tasks, we are to advance the reign of God. This means that, like the Baptist, we are to prepare the way of the Lord. We do not build our kingdom, but help to build the Kingdom of God. We learn to live each day with a "respectful detachment." We take seriously the call to love others and work for justice and peace. But we always know that there is a Kingdom not made by human hands. This world is not our lasting home. During the season of Advent we wait for the Child Jesus, and we hope for his return in glory.

Friday of the Second Week

Isaiah
48:17-19

The prophet offers a corrective insight to the Deuteronomic Principle. This principle stated that the virtuous were blessed by God with the good things of life. One had a large family, a successful business, and was blessed with good health. On the other hand, the evil person was cursed by God with misfortune, poverty and sickness. This led many people to judge others on the basis of appearances. The wealthy were morally superior to the poor. Yet the prophet indicates that appearances can deceive. Yahweh often chooses the lowly, the poor and the weak to carry out His plans. The reason being that the powerless do not boast in their abilities, but are made strong through God. The rich and powerful often boast of personal achievements, and forget all that Yahweh has done for them. The prophet indicates that those who remain faithful will prosper, their descendants will multiply, and their names will be remembered forever by God.

Matthew 11:16-19

The most difficult aspect of Jesus' message is the need to change. To hear the message of the Kingdom means that one can no longer live according to the old values and way of life. Through Jesus, all are made new. John the Baptizer came and preached austerity and repentance. The religious leaders called John "a madman." Jesus comes and calls the people to celebrate the good news of salvation. The wedding banquet has begun. The Pharisees call Jesus a glutton and a drunkard. Simply put, people don't want to change and will do everything to avoid it.

MISSION IMPOSSIBLE

Several years ago, there was a popular television series entitled *Mission Impossible*. In this season to be jolly, we may often feel that we are part of a "mission impossible"—trying to please everyone. Just think of all those presents we *must* buy in the hope of pleasing everyone from the postman (post-person?) to our in-laws. Early in life, we learn how important it is to please others. We must please parents, teachers, friends, spouses and bosses. We become "other-directed" and cue our behavior from the emotional rewards and punishments given by our "significant other." We may even legitimate this "pleasing others syndrome" by claiming that we are serving others and being kind. However, there is always the danger that we move from being a servant to a slave. Instead of doing for others out of love we do so out of compulsion, or from a fear of rejection if we don't live up to their expectations.

The prophet in our first reading is not concerned about pleasing others. He wants to teach them the way of the Lord. Such teaching requires discipline and fidelity. These are hard lessons. Yet they yield an abundant harvest. The commandments of the Lord serve as a guideline for a right relationship between God and others. If one is able to follow the teachings of the Lord, one will be prosperous and see vindication. The obedient person will be fruitful and never know want. Above all, those who follow the Lord will remain forever in the loving presence of God.

In our Gospel reading, we already see how impossible it is to please everyone. Not even Jesus could please all of the people all of the time. John the Baptist was given the mission of preparing the people for the birth of the Messiah. John called the people to repentance and conversion. The new creation was about to dawn. Many rejected John as a madman, and accused him of taking all the fun out of religion. Naturally since John was discredited as a person, his message could be dismissed with equal ease. People must want someone to proclaim good news that is unlike John's negative message. Right? Wrong. Jesus comes and fares no better.

Jesus comes to the people as the Good News of the Father calling people to celebrate the Kingdom. Sin and death will not have the last word. Through the birth of

Jesus, God has accepted totally and unconditionally all that is human. Yet people reject this, and call Jesus a glutton and a drunkard. Above all, he associates with tax collectors and those of ill repute. The good news of Jesus is bad news for those who want to hold onto the *status quo*. Jesus' message of love and forgiveness is bad news for the smug and self-righteous. The birth of Jesus is the completion of Israel's hope and consolation. The human heart must change and become one that responds to the Father. Yet change is so difficult and uncomfortable. Maybe the next prophet or Messiah will fare better.

Advent does not speak to us of "mission impossible," but of the unbounded love of God. Ours is not a God we must please. God doesn't want our accomplishments or success stories. The God who became flesh in Jesus wants much more than that. Our God wants each of us, so that He can give us life to the full. The real "mission impossible" is not in trying to please God or others, but in really believing that in Jesus God is totally for us. Hence we can be totally for God, by serving one another in love. This is the "mission possible" and the hope of this season.

Saturday of the Second Week

Sirach
48:1-4,
9-11

Ben Sirach is the great wise man of the Old Testament. This section is called "The Praise of the Fathers." Sirach goes deep into the memory and expectations associated with Elijah. Elijah was the great prophet of the Old Testament. He was taken up into Heaven in a chariot. He was so great because of his faith, that Yahweh would not let death touch him. Also, it was believed that Elijah would return from heaven in order to usher in the Messianic age. The day of the Lord will come and Elijah will prepare the people for it. Finally, Sirach recalls the heroes of Israel's history in order to provide a sense of earned pride. Israel does not have to feel inferior in comparison with Greek wisdom and culture. The Greeks have philosophy and worldly wisdom. Israel has the covenant and divine revelation. True wisdom comes to those who obey the will of Yahweh.

Matthew 17:10-13

As we saw in our reading from Sirach, the people were expecting the return of Elijah. He would usher in the Messianic age and prepare the people to worthily proclaim the Day of the Lord. Jesus indicates that Elijah has returned in the person of John the Baptist. However, many did not recognize him and refused to believe in his message of repentance and conversion. Jesus reminds the disciples that the Son of Man must suffer and be rejected by the people. It is of the utmost importance to keep the following in mind: the Messiah is also the Suffering Servant. The birth of Jesus also speaks of the cross and the tomb.

RECOGNITION

Psychologist Abraham Maslow (the developer of humanistic psychology) spent his entire life studying the healthy personality. Dr. Maslow wanted to know what qualities the healthy, integrated person possessed. He found that the self-actualized personality was able to satisfy basic needs. Needs begin on the biological level and ascend to the spiritual. The healthy person is one who has his basic needs satisfied—food, clothing, companionship and a whole host of self-esteem needs. The healthy personality is one which possesses a good self-concept and is recognized by others as worthwhile and acceptable. Simply put, we need recognition for mental health, and we need the acceptance of others in order to grow as a person. We know how full of life and joy we feel, when others recognize our work and value our person.

The wise man Sirach, in our first reading, appeals to Israel's waiting for the return of Elijah. Elijah was the prophet who was so loved by God that he was taken up into Heaven. Before the coming of the Day of the Lord, Elijah was to return from Heaven and prepare the people for the Messianic age. Unfortunately when Elijah does return in the person of John the Baptist, the people do not recognize him. Why? Because their expectations block their recognition of John as the herald of the Messiah and of Jesus as the Messiah. The people were looking for a great figure, riding on a chariot, surrounded by fire. Instead, they were presented with a voice crying in the wilderness to prepare the way of the Lord through repentance and conversion. John was rejected as a madman, and did not receive the recognition required. But those who accepted John were led to the Lamb who takes away sin and gives eternal life.

Jesus did not receive recognition as the Messiah and as the Good News of the Father. People wanted a Messiah who would drive out the Romans and reestablish the glory that was once King David's. Certainly Jesus, this carpenter's son, was not the One. He too is a madman. Worse, Jesus is a blasphemer in claiming to be the Son of God. Above all,

Jesus has the audacity to connect the Messiah with the Suffering Servant. The Messiah must suffer, be rejected by the leaders and die on a cross. This was not the kind of Messiah the people wanted. Yet those who recognize Jesus through faith (tax collectors, sinners, the powerless and the lonely) possess the joy of the Messianic age. They experience the joy which no one can take away.

Advent is a season which challenges us to recognize the gift of this holy time. God has come, out of love, into our world. He comes to tell us how much we are loved and how much we are meant for glory. Through the birth of this child, we have been totally and unconditionally accepted by God. This total acceptance gives us the courage to accept ourselves and others. We are liberated from the compulsion to compete with others in order to prove our self-worth. In Jesus, we are forever valued and cherished by God. God's recognition and love for us is never taken back. Again, the real issue is whether we have the wisdom to recognize the gift of Jesus. God's unbounded love comes in the form of a child, bringing words of peace and healing. This child will grow in grace and wisdom to become the man for others and the man of sorrows. The crib and the cross are God's ultimate gifts of love and hope. Do we recognize them? Do we experience them? Do we have the courage to accept them? If we do, then this season of love speaks to us of Easter as well, and of our hope of glory.

Immaculate Conception

**Genesis
3:9-15, 20**

The writer of Genesis presents us with the consequences of sin. Sin brings total alienation and the feeling of being separate and alone. Before sin, Adam and Eve gave the animals their names and were entrusted with the good creation. However, motivated by pride, sin entered our human condition and history. The result is estrangement. Humankind is separated from God, the ground of all unity. We are separated from ourselves and each other. We are alienated from nature, which now becomes an article for man to exploit. However, the living power of God is present even here. God will not forsake creation and humankind. We also have the promise of a redeemer who will reconcile all that has been torn asunder. The old creation will give way to the new creation with the coming of Jesus.

**Ephesians
1:3-6, 11-12**

Through the salvific mission of Jesus Christ, we are called to share eternal life with the Father. Through Jesus, we are given every spiritual blessing. The community formed in Jesus' name is to live a life of love and holiness. Certainly, Mary is the prime example of this call to holiness and love. Like Mary, our lives are to be a living testimony to what God has done for us in Christ. By saying our "yes in faith" to the Word made flesh, we are called to share in the very glory of God.

Luke
1:26-38

Among the major themes in Luke's Gospel, those of joy and the honored place of women rank high. Gabriel comes to announce that Mary is to be the mother of the Messiah. She is to rejoice at her high place in the plan of salvation history. Mary is blessed, full of grace, among women. By her faith, she will provide the human means for the Word to become flesh. In the midst of her confusion, she utters the words of every Christian, "I am the servant of the Lord. Let it be done to me as you say."

HAIL MARY!

How wonderful in the midst of our Advent preparation to celebrate this great feast of God's grace, of Mary as the model for the Church and each individual Christian, and as the hope of all creation. Let us interject a necessary word of caution. At times we can get carried away with the "glory side" of Mary (much as we do with the divinity of Jesus), forgetting her humanity. For it is the human flesh and blood of Mary that speaks so eloquently to our hearts. She is the lowly virgin whom God does great things to and through. She is the maidservant of the Lord, who is declared to be blessed and full of grace. Mary is most human, and certainly this accounts for a great deal of her influence on the Church and on the life of the Christian. Let us briefly examine three aspects of Mary.

1. The Immaculate Conception is the celebration of God's grace. The fullness of God's grace—as Paul says in Ephesians, "every spiritual blessing"—comes to rest in Mary. From the moment of her conception in the womb, Mary was to be a crucial factor in salvation history. Through her "yes" of faith, she would become the new Eve. She would be the new mother of the new creation. The disobedience and pride of the first Eve is replaced by the obedience and humility of Mary. In the words of Gabriel, "Blessed are you among women."

2. Mary is the model for the individual Christian and the Church as a whole. Mary, in fear and trembling, says she is the servant of the Lord and seeks to do His will. This is the essential creed of the Christian life: to be a servant of the Lord's word and to always seek to do His will. This was certainly not easy, and Mary knew much suffering from her unconditional "yes" of faith. Yet she is one with Jesus, who prays that the Father's will be done and not his. Mary is also the model for the Church, in that through her faith the Word becomes flesh. The Church is called to continue and make visible and concrete the loving Word of God for all creation. Mary and the Church join together in being the sacrament of Jesus. Through faith and love in Jesus the Christ, the world is offered a genuine hope for the future.

3. Mary is the hope of all creation. The Immaculate Conception speaks to us of the original meaning of creation and of its ultimate destiny. From the beginning, God created out of love and called all creation to share His life. However, through sin everything was altered. Creation, tainted by sin, was in need of a redeemer to usher in the new age. Mary's Immaculate Conception speaks to us of the beginning of this new age. She is the first one to experience

the work of Jesus as the New Being. Through God's grace she anticipates what will be offered to all by God through Jesus. Mary is our hope of that holiness and grace which leads to eternal life.

In the midst of our Advent anticipation, we celebrate the woman who was allowed to anticipate the saving work of Jesus. We celebrate the holiness of Mary and her great place in the history of salvation. In a real sense, we celebrate God's grace for each of us. Mary was a real human being just like ourselves. What God has done in Mary is offered to each of us. We are highly favored with the gift of faith in Jesus. There are times when we feel the grip of fear and anxiety as we struggle to live the gospel. Let us take strength from the words of the angel: "Do not fear, you have found favor with God"; and inspiration from the life and words of Mary: "I am the servant of the Lord. Let it be done to me as you say." Today we say, "Hail Mary!" We raise our voices in thanksgiving to God. For the Almighty has done great things and continues to do them for each of us.

Monday of the Third Week

Numbers 24:2-7 15-17

Israel is continuing its journey to the promised land. They must pass through Moab. The King of Moab, Balak, sends for Balaam to invoke a curse upon Israel. For Balak is fearful that Israel will settle in Moab and take control of the country. Balaam comes, but tells Balak that he can't be bought. He will speak what the Lord tells him. Rather than invoking a curse, Balaam pronounces a blessing on Israel. A star and a staff shall rise from Israel and they will be a mighty people. In this episode, we once again see the care of God for His people. Yahweh even uses the forces of destruction to aid Israel and give Him glory. The reading ends with a note of confidence: a mighty king (David) will arise and usher in a period of greatness in Israel's history.

Matthew 21:23-27

Jesus is doing the work of his Father by teaching in the Temple area. The religious authorities come to Jesus and want to know the basis of his authority to teach. Jesus refuses to answer their question, for they are only trying to trap him. Instead, he turns the question on the Pharisees.

Jesus wants to know whether John's baptism was human or divine. If they say it was human, the Pharisees will upset the people and lose power. If they say it was divine, then why didn't they believe in his message and repent? In order to avoid the consequences of Jesus' question, they plead ignorance. How true! For they are self-righteous and blind to the workings of God.

AUTHORITY

We Americans are by national character distrustful of authority. This distrust extends deep into our history, and has become part of our collective consciousness. As a nation, we were forged into being by throwing off the yoke of an oppressive colonial power. Revolution gave birth to this nation, conceived in liberty and offering to the world the last best hope of humankind. The Founding Fathers (were there any Founding Mothers?) were deeply suspicious of authority and its abuses. Our system of checks and balances is an attempt to see that no one branch of government gains absolute control over the state. In fact, the ultimate power of government is to remain in the hands of the governed. We place a limit on the number of years a president can serve. Power corrupts and absolute power corrupts absolutely. In our recent history, we have grown not only suspicious but cynical towards those in authority working for the public good. The turmoil of the 60's and Watergate have left permanent scars on our psyche. It has become part of the conventional wisdom that *all* those in authority only seek their own advantage, and will eventually come to misuse their position. Such cynicism is deadly for any community or society.

Our two Scripture readings speak to us of the proper exercise of authority. In our first reading, Yahweh's authority is exercised through His providential care for Israel. Balak is the king of Moab and he is afraid that the Israelites will remain in his country. He wants Balaam to pronounce a curse on Israel. However, Balaam is a "man whose eye is true" and who says what the Lord tells him. Hence, instead of a curse, Balaam pronounces a blessing and speaks of the coming glory of King David. This little episode is typical of Yahweh's relationship with Israel. He is the great and powerful Lord who created all things by His mighty word. Yet Yahweh never uses His power to destroy His people or make them slaves to His will. Rather, He is a compassionate and loving God who wants His people to be faithful and have life. The history of Israel is one of Yahweh acting on behalf of His people, always calling them to deeper levels of freedom, responsibility and love. The authority of Yahweh is one of care and love.

The authority and power of God reaches its perfection with the coming of Jesus. He is the compassionate power of God's love for all people. The Pharisees want to know from Jesus what the authority is by which he does what he does. Jesus does not answer, because they don't really desire an answer. The Pharisees are looking to trap Jesus and hold on to their power. But we know that the authority of Jesus is the authority and power of compassionate love. He comes into our world as the good news of salvation. The blind see, the lame walk and the poor have the gospel preached to them. God in Jesus has table-fellowship with sinners, outcasts, the powerless and the marginals. The authority of Jesus is found in doing the will of the Father in absolute obedience. The obedience of Jesus to the Father's will is done out of perfect love and freedom. The will of the Father is to reveal His name as LOVE. Jesus does this through his ministry.

The Christian life is a vocation to continue the ministry of Jesus—making the Father's love real in our everyday lives. Our authority is always one of service to others. This service is never done out of a desire to control or manipulate others. Christian service is not an attempt to satisfy our own needs at the expense of others. Rather, we are called to serve others out of love in order to liberate them for a fully human life. Christian service is the authority and power to help others realize their full potential as children of God.

On what authority do we go about loving and serving others? Our authority is Jesus, who said to us long ago, "By this all will know that you are my disciples, if you have love for one another."

Tuesday of the Third Week

Zephaniah
3:1-2, 9-13

The power of the prophet is that he speaks the word of the Lord. This is a tremendous responsibility, and one filled with danger. The prophet is often met with rejection and hostility. Death is the ultimate answer from those who refuse to listen. Zephaniah comes proclaiming the Lord's word of judgment and hope. Israel has not listened to God's word, and has not trusted in Him. Israel has rebelled against the covenant. There is no justice in the land and hence, no real peace. But Zephaniah also proclaims a word of hope and triumph. There will be a remnant in the land of those who turn to the Lord. This remnant will be faithful and obedient to the Lord. They will trust in the covenant and seek the Lord's justice. Then will true peace be established in the land. Joy will find a place in their hearts.

Matthew
21:28-32

Jesus tells the parable of the two sons. Each was told to work in the vineyard. One said yes, but didn't go. The other said no, but repented and went to work. It is this second son who does the father's will. So it is with the audience of Jesus. He comes to announce the gospel to all people. Unfortunately, the religious leaders do not accept Jesus as the Messiah. It is the tax collectors and prostitutes who repent and believe in Jesus. They are the ones who truly do the will of the Father. It is not enough to say words of obedience: one must act obediently.

THE DANGER OF LISTENING

On the side of every package of cigarettes, there is a warning: cigarette smoking may be dangerous to your health. Perhaps there should be a warning that reads: listening may be dangerous to your comfortable life style. We learn early how important it is to be a selective listener. We must learn to hear what we want to hear, and to ignore what is challenging to our taken-for-granted worldview. "I didn't hear you" is a familiar expression offered as an excuse for not responding. The child doesn't hear mother's instructions about being home for dinner. The student fails to hear the assignment and does poorly on the test. The boss's instructions go undone because no one really listened. In all of these instances and many others, selective listening becomes a way of dealing with others and with the uncomfortable aspects of life. After all, if we didn't hear the instructions or really understand what others want, we can't be held responsible. We remain free to do our own thing, all the while avoiding the responsibility that comes with living with others. Selective listening affects our spiritual life, as well.

The role of the prophet is to proclaim the Lord's word in and out of season. The duty of the people is to hear the word and respond in faith. Zephaniah has been preaching to Israel, but to no avail. Israel has turned her back on the covenant, has failed to trust in Yahweh and has allowed social injustice to corrupt the community. Above all, Israel "hears no voice." Why? Because Israel wants no correction. She has grown comfortable and complacent doing what she wants. Israel's relationship with God has become a taken-for-granted thing. Nothing more is required. However, the prophet reminds the people that the covenant is an ongoing relationship in which Israel is called to deeper levels of love and commitment. To hear the word of the Lord is a call to conversion and purification. God's word is never fruitless, even if many turn away or selectively listen. For God will lift up a remnant faithful to His word in all its splendor and power. Zephaniah reminds the people that there can be no peace and prosperity apart from the Lord. Only if Israel repents, seeks justice and opens her heart to the Lord's word, will healing occur.

The parable of Jesus concerning the two sons takes our discussion a step further. Not only must we hear the word of God, but we must put it into practice. God is never satisfied with lip service. He wants us to put His words into action. The smug and the self-righteous heard the good news of Jesus, but rejected it as absurd. They were sure of their own moral superiority, and of the moral inferiority of others. The morally superior talked a great deal about God and doing His will. Unfortunately, their words were bold but their deeds few. Their words got in the way of the Lord's word made flesh. Jesus came as God's Word of love and forgiveness. He came to proclaim a year of favor. All people were to share in God's love. The self-righteous would not accept this. How could tax collectors and prostitutes be on an equal footing with all the respectable folk? No way. Hence, many spent their time verbally sparring with Jesus, all the while avoiding the need to change and be reborn. It is the lowly and the outcast who hear the words of Jesus and welcome them with joy.

Advent is the season when we seek ways to increase our religious practice. This is certainly commendable. Yet, let us not get caught up in a compulsive prayer life. We can multiply words and say many things. We can pray more but enjoy it less. This could be because we say a great deal in the hope of not hearing what God wants of us. If we speak enough, we may not hear what God desires. And what better way to selectively listen, than by using prayer as a way to avoid the Lord's word? There needs to be a balance between listening and responding. Blessed is the one who hears the word and puts it into practice.

Wednesday of the Third Week

Isaiah
45:6-8,
18, 21-25

The lowest point in Israel's history was reached in 587 B.C. This was the year of the Babylonian Exile. The Temple in Jerusalem was destroyed and the people were taken off to Babylon. Try to imagine the depth of Israel's humiliation and sorrow. Furthermore, this pain is compounded by the realization that Israel has brought this fate on herself by disobedience, infidelity and social injustice. In the midst of this situation beyond hope, the prophets proclaim hope and the promise of restoration. This will be done through the power and mercy of Yahweh. The Lord will show just how powerful and faithful He is. Even though Israel rejects the Lord, the Lord will never turn completely from the covenant. When Israel comes to its senses and returns to the Lord, then will vindication and glory shine forth.

Luke
7:18-23

Our Gospel reading opens with a legal prescription. The testimony of two witnesses was required by law to establish truth. Two disciples are sent by John the Baptist to inquire as to the identity of Jesus. Jesus does not give a direct answer. Rather, he tells them to report to John what they have witnessed: The blind see, cripples walk, lepers are cured, the deaf hear, the dead are raised to life and the poor have the good news preached to them. All of these are signs of the imminent Kingdom of God present in Jesus. The Gospel reading ends on the theme of Christian discipleship: blest is the person who is able to respond in faith to Jesus. The stumbling-block will become the cornerstone.

WHAT'S MY LINE?

Several years ago, there was a popular television show entitled *What's My Line?* The premise of this show was fairly simple. Someone with an unusual occupation would be presented to a panel of celebrities. After a series of questions, they would try to determine just what the person did. More often than not, the panel failed. I suppose part of the popularity of the show was related to the unusualness of the guests. Also, we like to think that certain people look like they belong to certain occupations. Most of us are in rather routine jobs, and we find it fascinating to hear what others do to earn their daily bread. The Christian is involved in work. However, our work is not a career but a vocation. We are called to proclaim the love of God in our lives by the way in which we serve others. Our readings share further insights into our vocation.

The Old Testament speaks eloquently about the special mission of Israel in salvation history. Yahweh will call upon Israel to be a light to the nations for guidance unto the Lord. Through Israel's fidelity, obedience and justice, all the nations would come to praise the Lord. Unfortunately, Israel was not always faithful to this mission. The low point is reached with the Babylonian Exile in 587 B.C. Since Israel has suffered this traumatic event, does it mean that Yahweh is not a faithful and powerful God? Hardly. Yahweh always leaves Israel free to make decisions and experience the consequences. However, Yahweh's power is in His loving providence even in such dark moments. For the God who brought everything into existence will not abandon His people. Israel will be restored. This restoration will be a sign to all the nations of just how faithful God is. Even in times of national distress, through the Lord's grace Israel is fulfilling its mission—leading the nations to the praise of Yahweh.

John the Baptist sends two disciples to ask the perennial question of the Christian community: Is Jesus the Christ, the Messiah who is to come? Jesus does not answer their question with words or become indignant at their inquiry. Rather, Jesus appeals to the work he does. Through the ministry of Jesus the blind see, cripples walk, lepers are cured, the deaf hear, the dead are raised to life and the poor have the good news preached to them. The answer to John and his disciples is through an appeal to the work of Jesus. The lost sheep, the marginals, the outcasts are called to be the citizens of the Kingdom. The sinners and those in the grip of guilt are called to table-fellowship with the Messiah who comes to free us from sin and death. The identity of Jesus is intimately related to his mission—the one who is Life gives life to all who come to him in faith.

During Advent, we ask in a more urgent way what Jesus means for our daily lives and our ultimate destiny. This question transcends any other concern. It is the timeless yet always timely concern of the Christian and the Church. It is never enough to repeat what others have said. We must experience the person of Jesus for ourselves. We must come to know Jesus and his healing presence in our own lives. In our moments of blindness, weakness, deafness and sin we must experience the life-giving touch of Jesus. In the poverty of our human condition, we are challenged to let Jesus be our richness.

Advent is a good time to ask: Is Jesus really the Savior that I have come to know and accept? Has Jesus been born into my heart? If in the inmost corners of our being we can say yes, then we are blest. Jesus is not a stumbling-block, but the way and truth which leads to eternal life.

Thursday of the Third Week

Isaiah
54:1-10

How are we to understand Israel's condition after the Exile? The prophet uses some troubling imagery: Israel is barren, a wife forsaken and a widow. Israel has forsaken the covenant and now she must endure the fate she deserves. After all, Israel turned away from the Lord. She sought other gods and various political alliances as insurance against the future. Social injustice has become evident by a lack of concern for the poor. Yet, in the midst of such deserved punishment, come words of hope and unbounded love. The prophet tells the people not to fear. Israel shall not be disgraced, forgotten or left to die. On the contrary, Yahweh's love will never leave Israel. Granted, the Lord may be moved to anger over Israel's infidelity, but the love of God is great and everlasting. Yahweh is a God of great tenderness, enduring love and life. The covenant with Yahweh is one of peace, and is given by the God of mercy.

Luke 7:24-30

Once again, Jesus pays tribute to John the Baptist. He calls John the greatest man born of a woman. John is the last of the prophets to prepare the way of the Messiah. Jesus indicates that looks are deceiving. John was not what the world expected or wanted. John was not a man of luxury and splendor, but a man on fire with the word of God. John did his job well—for the people, even tax collectors, give praise to God. By contrast, the self-righteous (Pharisees and lawyers) rejected John and hence are closed to Jesus as the Messiah. But as great as John is, the person born into the Kingdom through the baptism of Jesus is greater.

COMMITMENT

A significant aspect of modern life is the overwhelming abundance of choice. From the selection of a career to the choice of a mate down to the choice of our toothpaste, the options seem to be without limit. The future is wide open and it is only our lack of effort which can cause a life of failure. Together with this multiplicity of choice is the belief that there is a corresponding increase in freedom. With more options, we are liberated for a number of self-determined futures. However, we have all experienced the paradox of freedom. True freedom occurs when we make a decision for someone or something. The authentic exercise of freedom comes with the elimination of options, and the commitment to a given course of action. Too many options can actually paralyze us into inaction. We know how frustrating it is to be confronted with a number of good desserts, too many nice dresses or several good television shows playing at the same time. We can't have them all, so we must decide. Yet here is the paradox. In the decision for one, I automatically eliminate all the others. Much of our unhappiness results from trying to consume and choose everything. We want to let nothing pass us by.

In the final analysis, the mature exercise of freedom comes when we choose one and forsake all others. Freedom and commitment are inseparable. Isaiah reminds the people how deep is Yahweh's commitment to and for them. Israel had broken the covenant and been unfaithful to the Lord. She has chased after other gods and various earthly powers in the hope of having it all. Israel wanted Yahweh and the lesser gods as well. Yet the covenant is an exclusive relationship: the Lord your God is one and you are to love Him with your whole being. Love, freedom and commitment cannot

be separated. Israel must be faithful to Yahweh unconditionally. Why? Because the commitment of Yahweh to Israel
is unconditional, absolute and irreversible. "My love shall
never leave you nor my covenant of peace be shaken."
Yahweh demands a total response to His total giving and
self-revelation.

The absolute self-giving of God is found in the person of
Jesus. In Jesus, God commits Himself in an absolute, total
and irreversible way. God freely and lovingly says "yes" to
our condition and history. This self-giving of God in Jesus
calls for a total, free response of love on our part. As we
know, many chose not to accept Jesus as the Messiah. The
self-righteous and the mighty chose to remain on their
thrones. The human person has the power to frustrate
God's will and plan. Our Gospel reading closes by saying
that the Pharisees and the lawyers failed to receive John's
baptism and "defeated God's plan in their regard." God
always respects our freedom. There can be no genuine
commitment in love without a free decision on the part of
each person. It is the common folk, sinners and tax collectors who respond to Jesus and the Good News. In the
poverty of their condition, God becomes their richness and
strength.

Advent is an excellent time to pause and reflect on the
absolute love commitment of God in Jesus to us. This season
reminds us of the unbounded love of God that is faithful
and healing. The commitment of God on our behalf is not
because of our power, goodness or achievement. Rather, it is
because we are in need of healing, peace and reconciliation
that the Word becomes flesh. St. Paul, in the letter to the
Romans, says that the proof of God's love for us is that while
we were sinners, God came in Jesus and died for us. Advent
is an opportune time to reach out to others. Most especially

to those who are poor in the eyes of the world. In freedom and love, we are called to baptize the worth and dignity of all people as images of God. There is always something more than physical appearances. The love commitment of God often comes in the most surprising ways: in a messenger crying in the wilderness; a child born in a manger; a man on the cross. In each of these, what do we really see?

Friday of the Third Week

Isaiah
56:1-3, 6-8

This part of the book of Isaiah is called "Third Isaiah." It is written after the Exile, when the people have returned to the land of the promise. The prophet issues a call to holiness and justice. The salvation of the Lord is about to burst forth. True happiness comes to the person who is faithful to the Lord and keeps the sabbath. The people have a responsibility to be holy, so others will be inspired by their example. The holiness and fidelity of the Israelites will lead others to worship the true God. The symbol of the Lord's holy mountain is used. This mountain will be one of prayer and pure worship. Salvation will be offered to all people, and the Jews living in the diaspora will be gathered together. The Lord desires all people to be saved.

John
5:33-36

Throughout the Fourth Gospel, there is a strong appeal to the Jewish legal tradition. The confrontation between Jesus and the Jews is often presented in a courtroom fashion. Jesus tells the Jews that John came as a witness to the truth by his preaching, fasting and prayers. For awhile, the people believed in John. However, they finally rejected him. Jesus comes with testimony that is greater than John's—namely, the very works of God. The actions of Jesus speak louder than words. Jesus appeals to three witnesses: John who spoke of him as the Lamb, the works that he does and most importantly, the mission given to him by the Father.

IS EVERYBODY HAPPY?

What a silly question. Of course we are happy. Who wouldn't be? We live longer. We have the highest standard of living in the history of humankind. Many diseases are no longer fatal. People possess an endless parade of opportunities for the enjoyment of life. The material comforts at our disposal have relieved us of much of the burdens of daily existence. Our work week has been greatly reduced. We have a superabundance of leisure time. The car and airplane have provided us with an abundance of freedom through mobility. All in all, things are pretty good in River City! Yet if we look deeply at the contemporary scene, we also notice a great deal of quiet—and not so quiet—desperation. We certainly have an abundance of the material goods of this world. However, nagging questions persist: What good does it do to live longer without a meaningful existence? How are we to creatively use the leisure time we have so much of? Does our mobility erode our sense of tradition and belonging? Are material comforts enough to insure human happiness?

Such questions are persistent and serious. The perspective of the Bible can prove helpful. The biblical testimony tells us that happiness is not something we achieve, but something we receive as a gift. Happiness and joy are not commodities to be had by the highest bidder. Rather, they are given by the good and gracious God in whose image we are made. The prophet Isaiah says that happiness comes to the one who seeks justice and does the will of God. There can be no true or lasting happiness apart from the will of God. What is it to do the will of God? The Bible says it is to seek after holiness all of one's life. Such holiness is not an escape from this world. Quite the opposite. We are to be concerned about nature and our needy neighbor, and about helping others to know the Lord. The happy person is a person of prayer. It is through seeking after justice, personal holiness, good example and prayer that we come to experience an inner joy which no one can remove.

In our Gospel reading, Jesus continues this theme with a much-needed note of caution. The happy and just one is the person who makes Christ present to others and who does the works of the Father. This was the mission of John and Jesus. The Baptist testified about Jesus. Jesus came to give life to all who believe in him. Jesus reveals the name of the Father as LOVE. The witness of John and the ministry of Jesus remind us that the Christian can expect opposition, rejection and even death. Holiness is not some magical exemption from suffering. In fact, to do the works of God and to seek this holiness is to find suffering. Yet we need not fear. For those who come in the name of the Lord will be given the strength to persevere through the Spirit. Like John, we are to be "a lamp, set aflame and burning bright."

Advent is a time when we experience much happiness and joy. Let us never lose sight of the reason for this season and its ultimate call to peace. This is the season when we prepare for the ultimate gift of God's love in the Word made flesh. Our joy and happiness come from doing what is just and right. We are at peace when we dedicate ourselves to doing the works of the Father—that is, the works of love. Let our life be a hymn to the Father's love for us. Let our life be a hymn to the love we have for one another. Love is the hymn of joy.

December 17

Genesis
49:2, 8, 10

This section from Genesis invites us into a conversation between Jacob and his sons. The sons of Jacob are promised that their descendants will continue to rule and stay in power. Furthermore, the Twelve Tribes will submit themselves to the rule of David, who is a warrior of courage and power. David (Judah) will be a ruler on whom the spirit of the Lord rests. He will be deserving of the obedience of all the tribes. What is of crucial importance is that God is a faithful God. He will not turn back on His covenant. The reign of David will be everlasting. Yahweh did not choose the powerful and the strong. Rather, the Lord chose Judah to be the instrument of universal salvation. Through Judah all people will come to know just how powerful, faithful and loving is Yahweh.

Matthew
1:1-17

The opening of Matthew's Gospel presents us with the genealogy of Jesus. Jesus is the Messiah, the one who is expected, who completes the Law and the prophets. He is the apex and perfection of salvation history. Matthew takes great care to relate Jesus Christ to David and the Patriarchs.

Matthew is writing for the Jewish-Christian community at Antioch. He wants to establish the authority of Jesus in light of Israel's expectation of the Messiah. Jesus was not the Messiah people expected. He did not come in the royal fashion hoped for. Rather, Jesus entered into the poverty of our condition. His message proved a stumbling-block to many. The cross and resurrection bring life to those who accept Jesus in faith.

ALL IN THE FAMILY

Ever since Alex Haley set out to discover his *Roots*, the fascination with genealogy and family trees has become a national compulsion—and a big business. What is it that has struck a responsive chord? Why have people in droves set out to trace their roots? There are many reasons. We would like to know if our DNA has a famous connection in the past. Maybe a king or some celebrity fell from the same tree that deposited us. Mr. Haley touched a responsive chord in seeking to find his roots. A sense of dignity and pride was most evident. But I suspect that the fascination with genealogies stems from the need we all have to belong. We need to be part of something larger than ourselves. The isolated ego must fit in with a reality that extends beyond itself. Genealogies and family trees speak to us of a community of love which can be traced over time, and which hopefully will extend into the future. The family tree gives us a sense of solidarity with others in facing the problems of existence. Just when we thought we didn't need traditions of the past, Mr. Haley searches for *Roots* and we all start digging.

Our two readings speak to us of the importance of roots and of belonging to a living tradition. Yahweh initiates a covenant with Abraham, and promises that his descendants will be as numerous as the stars. What's more crucial is that out of this covenant will come the Messiah, through whom all the nations will be saved and blessed. This covenant and promise will extend throughout history. Within the uncertainties and surprises, the tragedies and heroics of the human story, Yahweh will remain faithful. It is out of the tribe of Judah and the House of David that the Messiah-King will come to rule the peoples in justice and peace. No matter how difficult Israel's experiences over time, the Lord is steadfast in His word. Through this small and insignificant tribe, God will effect His saving will. All the nations will come together in the one family of humankind, under the peace of Yahweh.

St. Matthew begins his Gospel with the roots of Jesus. He wants to show that Jesus is part of this covenant story. In fact, he is the perfection and hope of the covenant. With the birth of Jesus, the new covenant is now written on the heart in spirit and truth. Jesus is a son of Abraham and a son of David. He does not come to do his own thing, but the will of the Father. Jesus proceeds from that great cloud of witnesses and faithful ones who rejoice at the coming of the Messiah. It is in the fullness of time, the completion of a tradition and the keeping of a promise that Jesus comes to announce the Good News of salvation.

Advent and Christmas are times when we draw closer to our families and loved ones. We seek out that intimate circle of significant others, who accept us unconditionally and love us for who we are and not for our achievements. These are the days in which we join with a community of love that speaks to us of the giftedness of life. Children come home from schools far away. We see friends and relations long forgotten. Good friends become dear ones. Those with whom we are at odds assume a different posture in our evaluations. It is a time of reconciliation and peace.

This season also speaks to us of that larger family and that future hope of humankind. In drawing close to our immediate family, we pause and lift a prayer for the unity of all peoples in peace. We long for that day in hope when all God's children will come to this holy mountain in prayer and rejoicing. The Tower of Babel stands as a symbol of our original fall and of the divisions that lead to violence and war. The crib in Bethlehem, the cross on Golgotha, and the Spirit on Pentecost speak to us of that day when we will be all in the family—the one family of God.

December 18

Jeremiah 23:5-8

From the perspective of the Old Testament, political authority is always a sacred trust. The king is the anointed one of the Lord, who must lead the people into the ways of justice and fidelity to the covenant. However, the kings of Judah have been poor leaders. They have led the people into injustice, and the result is a loss of peace. There can be no peace without justice. However, Yahweh will not be defeated. He will raise up a king who is wise and just. Through him, a descendant of David, Israel will live in prosperity, security and peace. The Lord once brought Israel out of the land of Egypt into a new land of milk and honey. The day is coming when the Lord will bring Israel back to the promised land from her exile in Babylon. This restoration will cause all the nations to praise Yahweh.

Matthew
1:18-24

Jesus is the completion of the promise, and the perfection of salvation history. The birth of Jesus the Christ comes, not through human achievements, but by the grace of God and the power of the Spirit. Jesus is a pure gift. He is the gift of salvation by which people are saved from sin and death. The virgin is to have a child and call him Emmanuel—"God is with us." In this child, God will be with and for His people. Throughout this passage, we are presented with Joseph as a key figure in God's plans. Joseph is the one who receives the revelation about the identity and mission of Jesus. In spite of the unusual circumstance, he accepts the dream and takes Mary into his house. Joseph, Mary and Jesus form the Holy Family.

SOMETHING NEW

We Americans have had a long love affair with the new. The first arrivals from Europe understood their passage as a New Exodus. God was leading this New Chosen People into a new promised land. God was establishing a new covenant with this people in this land, in the hopes of converting Europe, which had gone astray. Our cities and states are prefixed with "new"—New England, New York, New Jersey and New Hampshire, to name but a few. Much of early American literature glorified the new. Who is the American? He is the "new man" through whom God is doing mighty things. Part of the attraction of the new is the promise of liberation from the past, of starting all over. The new speaks to us of washing the slate clean and beginning again. We have another chance to get things right. The lure of the frontier blended with the new in our hopes of overcoming past failures. This time we will succeed.

Yet we know that none of us is really free from the past. Every new thing is in some way connected to the past. The past lives in every present and helps form every future. Part of the power of sin is its power to hold us captive through guilt. Our past sins are always before us. We can come to believe that there is no way out—hence, we despair. The prophet Jeremiah speaks of a new day when the Lord will raise up a righteous ruler from the house of David. This person will rule with justice and establish peace in the land. Yet the past is evoked in light of this future hope. The God of the Exodus is also the God of the Babylonian Exile and Restoration. Israel will continue to fall in and out of covenant relationship with Yahweh. The pull of sin is strong. Past failures have ways of hanging on in the hidden corners of our psyche (individual and collective). Sin leaves scars on the heart, which by ourselves we are powerless to heal. The truly new is beyond our poor powers to bring about. The really new comes to us as a gift.

With the birth of Jesus Christ, God does something truly, uniquely and ultimately new. Jesus is the new humanity, and ushers in the new creation. In Jesus, "God is with us" (Emmanuel) and for us totally and forever. He is the revelation of God as suffering, enduring love. Jesus is the revelation of the truly human. Through Jesus we have revealed to us what we are meant to be as *imago Dei* and *imago Christi*. He shows us the way into the new creation—by loving God and serving our neighbor. In Jesus the power of sin, guilt and death are swallowed up in the victory of the Cross and the empty tomb. He is the one who takes all the power of the past and the old self, and redeems it through suffering love. The birth of Jesus speaks to us of the new covenant, in which we are born into eternal life.

There is a wonderful Jewish saying that is connected with the birth of every child. It says that as long as a child is born, there is hope. Each new child is a signal that God has not yet given up on the world. Each baby speaks to us of God's faithful love. How true this is, when applied to the One born in a stable long ago. With the birth of Jesus, God is with and for us. The faithful love of God becomes visible in the person of Jesus. In him, God is doing something really and lastingly new. The birth of Jesus is the liberation from the power of sin. Through baptism into Jesus, each of us is called to live in the newness of life—and to live this new life in Jesus now!

December 19

Judges
13:2-7, 24-25

Once again we are invited into the wondrous and fruitful surprises of Yahweh—the Lord of Life. The wife of Manoah is barren. The angel of the Lord announces that she will bear a son. He will be a man consecrated to the Lord from the moment of his conception. He is a true gift of the gracious Lord. Hence, he must be kept pure and find strength only in the Lord. The Israelites continue to disobey Yahweh and are delivered up to the Philistines. However, Yahweh will use this son of

Manoah to liberate the Israelites. This son is Samson. The spirit of the Lord is with Samson so that he will be faithful to the mission given by God.

Luke 1:5-25

In one of our earlier readings (Mt 17:10-13, Saturday of the Second Week), we saw that it was believed that the prophet Elijah would return to prepare for the coming of the Messiah. John the Baptist carries out this mission of Elijah. He is the voice of one crying in the wilderness and calling the people to prepare themselves for the Messiah. Once again, we see the power of God's love as giving life when all hope is lost. John is a child given by God to Elizabeth, who is barren, and Zechariah. John is a source of great joy and gladness to his parents. He will be more. It is John who will prepare a people who are well-disposed to receive the Word. Like Samson in our first reading, John is consecrated to the Lord from conception and will remain faithful to his mission. Both Samson and John give up their lives in the service of the Lord. In so doing, both come to experience eternal life.

STRENGTH

Strength has many forms. The most obvious is physical strength. Flexing bulging muscles and "pumping iron" makes one the most sought-after man (it should be added that women are getting into the act as well) on the beach. No one will kick sand in your face! There is emotional strength, whereby we are able to keep a "stiff upper lip" and tough it out. We won't cry or make a scene. In the midst of tragedy and fear, we carry on and make the best of any situation. Perhaps the most sought-after is economic strength. The almighty dollar and the rising GNP are the golden calves which attract so many to their altars. In this "dangerous decade," we want military superiority. America wants more bang for the buck, and Russia wants more rubble for the ruble. Horses, chariots and charioteers have been replaced by ICBM's, SS-20's and cruise missiles. All these forms of strength are limited, and in time pass away. True strength is found in the inward disposition of the soul which resolutely seeks the Lord's will.

The book of Judges speaks to us of the famous strong-man, Samson. His physical strength is obvious. He can defeat any foe, and even kill wild animals with his bare hands. Yet the real strength of Samson comes from the spirit of the Lord. He is consecrated to God from conception. Through God's life-giving power, the barren are made fruitful. Samson's conception, as well as his strength, is derived from the Lord. Luke's account of the birth of John the Baptist is similar. Elizabeth is barren, and has lost hope of having a child. However, not only will Elizabeth conceive, but her son will fulfill the mission of Elijah and prepare the way of the Messiah. John is filled with the Holy Spirit from the moment of conception. Samson grows in strength to deliver the Israelites from the Philistines. John grows in the Spirit, and proclaims the One who will be Savior to the whole world.

In both of our Scripture readings, we see that strength and salvation are divine gifts. The parents of Samson and John had given up the hope of having a child. God works through the weak, and makes them strong. He calls those who have reached the end of *their* resources to be part of salvation history. The barren are now fruitful, and those who were in captivity are now brought into freedom. In the person of Jesus, we are liberated from the ultimate enemy of humankind—sin. However, no one earns salvation. Jesus as the Good News of the Father is offered to us as pure gift. Through Jesus, we are accepted unconditionally and offered the hope of eternal life. Real strength is the ability to accept the unconditional acceptance offered to us in Jesus.

Advent speaks to us of God's power. Yet the power and strength of the Lord are found in the most unlikely way—a child born in a crib. God's strength is His embracing the poverty and weakness of our human, all too human condition. God in Jesus does not cling to the divine status, but empties Himself out of love into our humanity. God's strength is the power to be with and for us completely and forever. He does not want our strength, achievements, trophies or sources of personal power. God wants a receptive heart where the Holy Spirit can dwell in truth. It is at the moment of greatest human weakness that God is strong. Samson will be killed, but the Philistines are destroyed and Israel is liberated. John the Baptist will be beheaded, but not without preparing the way for Jesus. Jesus' death on the cross is really the hour of victory. In our own personal moments of weakness and inadequacy, let us pray for the courage to turn to the Lord who is our strength.

December 20

Isaiah
7:10-14

The year is 735 B.C. It is a time of decision for Ahaz, the king of Judah. Ahaz is the legitimate king, but he is weak and lacking in faith. Assyria is the most powerful of nations at this time. The rulers of Aram and Israel request Ahaz to join them in an alliance against Assyria. He rejects this request. The kings of Aram and Israel plan to attack Judah. Out of fear, Ahaz seeks the help of Assyria. The prophet Isaiah comes to Ahaz and confronts him with the covenant: Ahaz must place his trust in the Lord and not some political alliance with Assyria. The Lord's love is everlasting, while political power fades. Israel and Aram will be destroyed, but the Lord will protect Judah. Isaiah tells Ahaz to ask for a sign to confirm the truth of the prophet's words. Ahaz tries to sidestep the issue by saying that it is not right to test the Lord. Isaiah tells Ahaz he will receive a sign—a virgin will give birth to a son named Immanuel. This sign means that God is with His people. Hence, Ahaz must trust in God and not in Assyria or in worldly power.

**Luke
1:26-38**

In yesterday's reading, we considered the conception and birth of John the Baptist. Now Luke presents the birth of the Messiah and the obedience of Mary. The child of Mary will be called Jesus, which means "Yahweh is salvation." Yahweh will save from their sins all who accept Jesus in faith. Mary holds a special place in Luke's Gospel. She is the human instrument through whom the Word becomes flesh. Mary is the model Christian, because she hears the Word of God and responds totally in faith. She is a woman filled with

grace, whose life speaks to every genera-
tion of the great things God has done
through her for all humankind.

TRUST IN THE LORD

An essential aspect of interpersonal and social life is
trust. Without trust, our relationships are burdens rather
than joys. Without trust, no society can long endure.
Harvard psychiatrist Erik Erikson lists basic trust as the first
and most indispensable element in the formation of a
healthy personality. If the child experiences his or her envi-
ronment as safe and loving, then trust grows and so does the
child. If, on the other hand, the home is lacking in love and
security then trust is not formed and neither is the healthy
psyche. Many psychologists believe that without basic trust
in a person's early years, the damage is permanent. Lack of
basic trust leaves the person in a state of permanent insecu-
rity, which affects all aspects of one's interpersonal life.

Basic trust is not only essential for individual well-being;
it is essential for the well-being of a community and society.
Israel's basic trust stems from its relationship to Yahweh
through the covenant. Unfortunately, Israel is less than
faithful to this covenant of trust. The results are tragic: war,
division, exile and bondage. But Yahweh does not abandon
His people. Israel is slow to grow into total trust of the Lord.
The episode from Isaiah is classic. Ahaz is fearful of attack
from the kings of Israel and Aram. Instead of trusting in the
Lord, he turns to his own designs and to a political alliance
with Assyria. Isaiah announces the necessity of trusting in
the Lord. Political alliances fail and military power fades,
but the word of the Lord endures and one can trust in it
completely. The Lord never fails!

St. Luke presents Mary as the woman of perfect trust. The angel Gabriel announces to Mary that she will give birth to a son, and name him Jesus. This son will be born through the power of the Spirit. Jesus is the Son of God who comes to liberate humankind from sin and death. We need to be clear about this: Mary was very human, and she was filled with anxiety. However, she did not allow this fear to determine her response. She transcended her fear and pronounced the words of faith, "Let it be done to me as you say." Mary was able to give her response of faith to the Lord, because her whole life had been one of trusting in God. This moment in Mary's life is a culmination of all that has gone before. Mary in her Immaculate Conception was filled with the grace of God's presence. Her Assumption into heaven is the culmination of a life lived in total faith and trust in the Lord's word.

Advent is a good time to examine our lives and see in whom we place our trust. It is a good time to reflect on our national and social life in terms of fidelity to God's love and concern for social justice. Are we, as a nation, generous and responsive to the needs of the poor and the powerless? Do we seek to build social structures which enhance human life, and free people to live with dignity and hope? Do we place our trust and hope in the Lord, rather than in worldly power and principalities? On a personal level, do we follow Mary as a servant of the Lord in keeping His word? Is our life one in which God's word is met with a receptive and trusting heart?

These are weighty questions, which demand a careful answer. Our life each day, and in its totality, is a response to these questions. Let us pray for the courage to trust in the Lord all of our days. The Lord is faithful, and we shall never be abandoned or disappointed.

December 21

Zephaniah
3:14-18

This reading from Zephaniah certainly captures the mood of the season. Israel is to shout for joy, sing and be glad—for salvation is at hand. Israel need not give in to fear and sadness. The Lord has removed the judgment against her. Yahweh will be her ruler, and He is always faithful to the covenant. The Lord Himself will be filled with joy at Israel's recovery. The Lord's love will recreate in Israel a responsive heart. Sorrow gives way to the joyful song.

OR

Song of Songs
2:8-14

What is the best way to describe the relationship between Yahweh and Israel? Passionate love. This love is one that renews the partners and overcomes the hurts of the past. The love of Yahweh and Israel is one that overcomes the barrenness of many winters. Love is associated with spring and the bursting forth of new life. This passionate love drives one to be with the beloved. It excites and uplifts. Love enhances our lives and brings forth every good quality.

Luke
1:39-45

After the Annunciation, Mary goes in haste to see Elizabeth. The two great figures of salvation history, John and Jesus, along with their mothers, converge in our Gospel reading. Mary, the mother of the Messiah, does not stand on ceremony. She

is a true disciple, and goes to rejoice with
Elizabeth. When Mary arrives, the baby in
Elizabeth's womb stirs with joy. Elizabeth
sings her praise of Mary. Mary is blessed
among women, because she trusted and
totally believed in God's Word. Very soon
the Word will be born, announcing the
good news of salvation.

JOY

Among the many criticisms directed against religion, the
charge of joylessness is most serious. This charge comes
from friend and foe alike. St. Teresa prayed to be delivered
from "gloomy saints." Teresa knew that it is not enough to
follow the letter of the law. It is the spirit that gives life.
Holiness needs to be humanly attractive, by being part of a
fully-alive human being. Jesus reminds his disciples that
when fasting, one should look as if one were not fasting. The
atheistic philosopher Friedrich Nietzsche was the son of a
Lutheran minister. After services he used to ask his sisters,
"Why don't you Christians look more redeemed?" Out of
the mouth of a child and an atheist! The question is essential: Why do Christians, who are called to be the experts at
joy and play, have so much trouble giving up doom and
gloom? Jesus reminds the disciples that there can be no
mourning when the bridegroom is with them. He even
compares the Kingdom of Heaven to a wedding banquet.
The good red wine will flow without end. Celebration is the
order of the day.

Yet having said all this, the question of Nietzsche
persists: Why do we have so much trouble with joy and
celebration? Essentially, we are afraid that having a good
time or smiling is a sign that one does not take life seriously.

We can't afford to celebrate when sin is so evident. Also, how can we be so insensitive to the hurts and pains of so many who lack the basic necessities for a human life? Without denying sin or trivializing the needs of the poor, the Christian brings hope, celebration and mirth to these situations. In fact, it is through hope and joy that we roll up our sleeves and help redeem and transform the present conditions of sin and suffering. One of our weapons against sin and suffering is the indispensable ingredient of joy.

Our three readings speak to us of the essential aspects of true joy. Joy is internal, a gift to be given: it comes from the Holy Spirit. A word about it would be helpful.

1. Joy is internal. Ultimately, we cannot acquire joy through the accumulation of material things. We may come to experience pleasure, but not joy. Pleasure is always in danger of slipping into trivia. Hence, there is the constant need to acquire more things in order to insure more pleasure. Pleasure does not lead one to peace, but rather to internal conflict and a restless spirit which never seems to have enough. In the Song of Songs, love produces the joy of life. Zephaniah calls Israel to find true joy in the covenant relationship with Yahweh. Joy comes to those who have the new covenant written in their heart. Both Elizabeth and Mary are filled with God's grace that brings forth new life.

2. Joy is a gift that must be given. The surest way to destroy joy is to keep it as a possession. Joy becomes real and enhanced when we share it with others. We also share in the joy of others, and rejoice with those who rejoice. The lovers in the Song of Songs must share the gift and joy of their love. Love and joy fill one with the desire to be with the beloved. Israel cannot keep the covenant to herself. Through Israel, all nations are called to experience Yahweh's salvation and peace. Mary goes in haste to be with Elizabeth and share in

her joy. Mary and Elizabeth were both filled with the Holy Spirit, and the life each carried would play its part in the salvation of the world.

3. Finally, joy comes from the indwelling of the Holy Spirit. The Spirit liberates us to give up the fear which drives out love. The Spirit of Yahweh comes to Israel, and renews her in the covenant. No longer will Israel have to turn to worldly illusions for joy. The presence of the Spirit enables the people to shout for joy and sing with festive voices to the Lord. Both Elizabeth and Mary are filled with the Holy Spirit. The barren one breaks into song, for the Lord brings forth life in the most unexpected ways. In the Virgin's total response of faith to God's Word, she becomes the most blest among women. Mary trusted the Lord completely.

There is a timeless quality and challenge about Nietzsche's question. The Christian cannot indulge in self-pity and gloom. There is simply too much to do and be. The birth of Jesus (along with his death and resurrection) is a permanent reminder that life is stronger than death. Hope will not be vanquished by despair. We may persist in our gloomy ways, and go about looking unredeemed. But please don't blame it on the writer of the Song of Songs, or on Zephaniah, Mary or Jesus. Let us place the blame where it belongs—on our free decision to hold the Spirit at a distance. Yet Yahweh and Jesus won't give up easily. We will have to work awfully hard to suppress joy. Maybe we will even succeed. However, what a surprise when we arrive in heaven and find everyone laughing! What then?

December 22

1 Samuel	Once again, the Bible speaks to us of the
1:24-28	barren bringing forth life. Sarah brought

forth Isaac. Samson and John the Baptist were conceived by women who had only human reproach for their lack of fruitfulness. But through the power of God's grace, new and unexpected things are accomplished. God is the giver of life to those who are open to receive. So it is with Samuel. He is born to a barren woman—Hannah. She prayed that if God gave her a son, he would be dedicated to the Lord's service forever (a perpetual nazirite). At the prescribed time, Hannah brings Samuel to the Temple at Shiloh and offers him to Eli the priest. Eli witnesses to her fidelity and accepts the child.

Luke
1:45-56

St. Luke recounts one of the most stirring and powerful proclamations of Mary. The Magnificat is a hymn of total praise to God for all He has done through Mary for the whole world. God is a faithful God, and He has kept His word of promise to Abraham and the succeeding generations of the covenant. The greatness of God is that He chooses the lowly and makes them strong. God seeks out the poor of the earth so that He can be their richness. Mary is the lowly servant of the Lord, who will be remembered as blessed for all times. In the Old Testament, Yahweh was the Lord who did mighty deeds on behalf of His people. Now, in the fullness of time, the mightiest of all deeds is done—the Word becomes flesh! In the child Jesus, the Good News of salvation is given visible expression.

THE MAGNIFICAT

Throughout the Scriptures, both Old and New Testaments, the picture presented to us is rather unnerving—He is the Lord of surprises and of the unexpected. Just when we think we have everything figured out and planned, along comes a new request or revelation that upsets our all-too-neat construction of God, self, others and the world. Israel is chosen to be the Lord's own. This "nothing special people" will be a light to the nations and a blessing to all peoples. No matter how often the covenant is broken, Yahweh continues to call forth a remnant of hope to continue the mission of salvation. In the New Testament, Jesus tells parables which shock the well-ordered world of the self-righteous. There are good Samaritans, tax collectors and publicans. God is a living Father who hears the prayers of the lowly and responds with love. The dedicated Saul must be blinded before he can see and become Paul the Apostle to the Gentiles. The God of Sinai and a crib in Bethlehem won't be confined by our expectations.

St. Luke's Gospel recounts the beautiful hymn of praise offered by Mary—the Magnificat. Throughout this hymn, the God of the unexpected is given praise and thanksgiving. The hymn can be divided into three sections. The Lord's greatness in relationship to Mary and the conceiving of Jesus. The power of the Lord in opposing the principalities and powers of this world. And thirdly, the mercy of the Lord in His relationship with Israel.

The whole being of Mary is a continual hymn of praise to what God has done for her. Mary is the Mother of the Messiah, and plays a most special role in salvation history. Mary is filled with a deep sense of joy and gratitude for the coming of the Savior. She is ever mindful of her true condition: lowly and humble. Yet it is through her lowliness that all generations come to call her blessed. The mighty deeds of God find expression through Mary's obedience—in contrast to the disobedience and pride of Eve in the Garden of Eden. The very essence of God is holiness. This holiness is extended through mercy to all who reverence the Lord's name.

However, many do not reverence the Lord's name. The self-righteous and worldly-powerful seek their own will, rather than the Lord's designs. Hence, the wisdom of the proud is thrown into confusion. The Tower of Babel indicates the idolatrous aspects of worldly wisdom and lack of trust in the Lord. The mighty and powerful are removed from their thrones of wealth and privilege. Instead, it is the lowly and the wretched of the earth who are raised up by God. Here we see the "transvaluation of values." Worldly power and success mean nothing in the Kingdom of God. Only a pure heart that seeks happiness and peace in the Lord will suffice. The rich and powerful are sent away empty. Their god is an idol who neither satisfies nor gives eternal life.

Finally, the Lord is faithful and merciful to His servant Israel. Yahweh made a covenant with Abraham long ago. Even though Israel has been less than faithful, Yahweh never falters. Through it all, the Lord suffers with Israel's growing pains, temptations and sins. The Lord also rejoices with Israel's growth in the covenant. He never gives up, and will not allow His people to give up. Fidelity is crucial!

The Magnificat is a hymn of praise and thanksgiving for the greatness, power and mercy of our God. The Magnificat also speaks to us of the surprises that God has in store for each of us. Israel, Mary and the poor are very unlikely characters for the story of salvation. Yet God chooses them, and never goes back on the promise or the gift. This season is one of ultimate surprise—God becomes human in a child. Not too many were ready for that (once again, the unlikely —shepherds and animals). Remember, we said that this God is like no other. To fall into His hands is a rather frightening thing. I wonder what He's got up His sleeve next? I wonder what He's got in store for me and *you*?

December 23

Malachi
3:1-4,
23-24

The terrible experience of the Exile is over. The people have been restored to the land. However, evil once again flourishes. In fact, those who exploit the poor and the lowly seem to prosper. How can this be? Isn't God just and caring for His people? Of course. The Lord is going to send his messenger to prepare the people for the Messiah. Malachi asks a troubling question: Who can endure the coming of the Messiah? For the Messiah comes to call the people to holiness and to turn away from sin. Elijah will return to prepare the people, but first and foremost the priests (sons of Levi) must be cleansed of sin. This is so that they can offer worthy sacrifices. The day of the Lord will result in reconciliation and unity. Those who re-fuse will be doomed.

Luke
1:57-66

Luke presents the birth of John the Baptist. The Lord's promise to Elizabeth and Zechariah has been kept with the birth of John. John is a source of joy to all who

come to his circumcision. In time, John
will rejoice and help many to rejoice at the
coming of Jesus. "John" is the name given
to the child by his parents as part of the
angel's revelation. The name means
"Yahweh has shown favor." Zechariah is
now able to speak, and he offers praise to
God. Those present are filled with awe,
and begin to wonder what role this child
will play in the Lord's service.

THE ETERNAL YES

Among the words that cause us a great deal of uneasi-
ness, the word "commitment" must rank high. This is especially true when we speak of a perpetual or unconditional
commitment. We wonder if claims to our allegiance can
have this timeless quality. After all, so much of modern life is
characterized by change and the subsequent loss of permanence. It seems so unrealistic to demand that a young couple
pledge their life and love to each other forever. Equally
suspect is the demand by the Church that one say "yes" to
Jesus Christ perpetually as a priest, brother or sister. So
much of life changes. The person that I am on a given day is
different at another time. New experiences and moods
change me. Commitments are of short duration. Life becomes a series of free-floating encounters of the most super-
ficial kind. Hence, perpetual vows, nuptial promises and
permanent commitments are part of a bygone age. Today
we live life in "the fast lane," and this results in a loss of
permanence.

While not wanting to deny the validity of the above
description, we can also say that there are other ways of
being in the world. Permanence, perpetual commitments
and vows can (however difficult) be accepted with a certain

degree of authenticity. The readings of today invite us to reflect on just such a possibility. The prophet Malachi assures the people that, amid the confusion and tragedy of history, one thing is constant—the love of God for His people. The Israelites have wavered many times. Their "yes" to the covenant has known many "maybes" and downright "noes." But Yahweh's word is always *yes*. *Yes* to the covenant and *yes* to Israel as she is and is meant to be. Notice that within the flux of history, the love of God is steadfast and unchanging. The power of God's love is His ability to creatively respond to the free decisions of Israel. The wisdom of God's love is His ability to draw every drop of goodness from each situation, and reoffer it to Israel as an opportunity to grow in the covenant.

God's commitment to Israel will reach a climax with the preaching of John and the birth of Jesus. Elizabeth, who was barren, would give birth to a son. This son would assume the role of Elijah, and prepare the people for the coming Messiah. God made a commitment to Elizabeth, and He did not go back on His promise. St. Luke recounts the birth of John, and the joy that filled all who were present. The name "John" means "Yahweh has shown favor." Yahweh has been faithful to His promise. What will this child be? John will be the herald who comes to prepare a people well-disposed to receive the Word made flesh.

Is it still possible to say "yes" to God and others in a permanent way? The joy of this season and the mystery of the Incarnation respond in the affirmative. The Incarnation is God's eternal, unconditional and total "yes" to each of us. In Jesus, God accepts each of us without reservation or precondition. This unbounded acceptance by God allows us to accept ourselves, and to say "yes" to the person we are and the one we hope to become. Having experienced the eternal "yes" of God for us (and also self-acceptance), we are now free to accept and commit ourselves to others. None of this is easy, or achieved by some magical technique. Rather, all this is a gift that we can only receive through faith. But that's alright. Isn't this what Advent and Christmas are all about—preparing ourselves to receive the Gift that no one can take from us?

December 24

2 Samuel
7:1-5,
8-11, 16

David has been successful in combat, and has become famous and rich. Unfortunately, David thinks all this is the result of his own efforts. He is an achiever. Now one last thing remains: David will build the Lord a temple. This temple or house becomes one more achievement for David. Nathan the prophet, after a vision, tells David that it is the Lord who will build a house and a kingdom for him. The house of David will be everlasting. Nathan reminds David that he was rather lowly when the Lord selected him to lead Israel. It was not David who defeated the armies opposed to Israel, but Yahweh. It is Yahweh who has made David's name famous throughout the world. Now Yahweh will show just how great He is, for David's house and kingdom will endure forever. God is faithful, and it will be so.

Luke
1:67-79

St. Luke presents for our consideration the powerful hymn of Zechariah. This hymn is one of praise for the God of Israel who is faithful to the covenant and who will send the Messiah. Yahweh is a God who cares and is involved in the history of Israel. It is through the house of David that the Messiah will emerge, and the prophets continue to remind the people of God's fidelity and of their need to be faithful. The enemies of Israel would be overcome. The covenant with Abraham will be completed with the coming of the Messiah. The Messiah will come to give the people the good news of salvation. The day of the Lord will be one of kindness and mercy. Those who respond to the Messiah with faith will come to know true and lasting peace.

DOUBT AND FAITH

Modern philosophy began with the thought of René Descartes (1596-1650). Descartes' philosophy was built on doubt, and sought to end in certainty. Through the use of the methods of mathematics, Descartes hoped to remove the uncertainty and confusion he found in philosophy. American philosophy was begun by Charles Sanders Peirce (1839-1914), who also appealed to the "irritation of doubt" in the fixing of one's beliefs. Doubt not only initiated our ideas, but also kept our beliefs from assuming a permanence they didn't deserve. Both Descartes and Peirce sought to use doubt in a constructive way. In many ways, the modern mind accepts doubt as a taken-for-granted part of the world. Yet doubt can have a serious effect on the believer. Often, we feel that to doubt is to be unfaithful. Doubt is seen as the enemy of religion and our relationship with God. However, might it not be possible that we, too, may constructively use doubt in the development of a more mature faith? Let's try by opening ourselves to the hymn of Zechariah.

When the angel announced to Zechariah that Elizabeth would bear a son, he doubted. He reminds the angel Gabriel that he is an old man, and that Elizabeth is also up in age. Gabriel tells Zechariah that he will be unable to speak until the child is born. However, Zechariah does not despair or give in to this doubt. Rather, he is able to transform doubt into faith. His tongue is set free, and his words of distrust become a hymn to the fidelity of the Lord. The hymn of Zechariah can be divided into three parts: the saving presence of God in Israel's history; the need for the people to respond with trust; and the sending of the Messiah as the One who liberates humankind from sin and death. Let us reflect on each of these aspects.

1. Yahweh is not an absent or uninvolved God. He is the Lord of history, and is actively at work in the struggles and concerns of His creation. The Sinai experience is a perpetual reminder that God *cares*, and expects His people to care and respond to His love. Yahweh is a jealous God, whose love is exclusive and passionate. Zechariah blesses the Lord who saved Israel through the Exodus, established the house of David and sent the prophets to call the people to holiness. Above all, Yahweh is a merciful and faithful God who keeps the covenant with Abraham through all the trials and difficulties of Israel's history.

2. If Yahweh is a faithful, compassionate and merciful God, Israel is to be a people made in His image and likeness. God is the very essence of holiness, and the people He has saved, liberated and made a covenant with must be holy as well. The covenant between Yahweh and Israel is a covenant which requires a commitment on the part of the people. The covenant of Yahweh is everlasting, and Israel must serve the Lord in a proper way forever.

3. The moment of God's fidelity and love is totally revealed in the person of Jesus. It is Zechariah's son who will have the privilege to proclaim the coming of the Messiah. John is the prophet who is sent to prepare the way of the Lord. Specifically, the people are called to be baptized and repent of their sins. The rough spots and hollow places must be smoothed over and filled in for the coming Messiah. The Messiah comes to liberate the people from their ultimate enemies: sin and death. The graciousness of God is made tangible in this child. Darkness gives way to light; hope overcomes despair; and strife is changed into a lasting peace. All of this is God's work as a pure gift to us.

We see, in this great hymn, a man whose doubt has been turned into joy and trust. Zechariah doubted, but he was not fixed in his doubt. Through grace and his free response, Zechariah's tongue is now able to praise God. Words of doubt are now transformed into a hymn of praise to our God. Jesus found the Pharisees so difficult because of their lack of faith. They had little faith because they had little doubt! They were self-righteous and self-certain in their own perfection. The grace of God, with its creative presence, could find no room in the inn of their hearts. It is the publicans, sinners and the lowly who come to true faith. They have doubts! How many and deep are their doubts! Yet the spark of faith burns. The preaching of John and the presence of Jesus fan that spark into a flame. This flame becomes a light which shines in the darkness. Each of our flames of faith become united with the Light who alone gives life. The Light of Life is near. Let us make Him welcome in the deepest corners of our being.

COME LORD JESUS!

I have no doubt that the discomfort of sitting on
one horn of a dilemma may awaken lively hopes of
the cushioned ease its alternative horn affords;
but the hopes are delusive. Sit there, and the horn
will presently enter your soul.
(*Faith and Speculation*, p. 119).

These words by Austin Farrer speak to us of the ultimate
dilemma and paradox of the Christian way—namely, "the
Word became flesh." There is a danger that we can become
too comfortable and familiar with the mystery of the Incarnation. God taking on a human face in Jesus can become
part of our taken-for-granted religious furniture. Unfortunately, a good deal of dust settles which blunts the splendor
of our furniture and our religious convictions. The preced-
ing meditations have been presented with the hope that
both the author and the reader will have done some spring
cleaning in the midst of winter's snow.

An essential part of this season is the challenge to wrestle
with the mystery of God's unbounded love. To appreciate
this season is to be comfortable with mystery. Here is the
rub, so to speak: being comfortable with mystery. Mystery is
often an abused religious concept. Whatever cannot be ex-
plained is dumped into the category of mystery. Unfortunately, mystery becomes meaningless and threadbare. However, the misuse of something is no argument against its

proper usage. Mystery is the fullness of reality and a superabundance of meaning. Hence, mystery is not something we can grasp and analyze through the scientific method. Rather, mystery is something which grasps us and which can only be known through the use of symbols, models, and the insights of the poet, artist and storyteller. Mystery is revealed to those who become comfortable and reverential with silence, Being and time. Mystery is seldom, if ever, revealed to those who approach the world through the imperial intellect and the will to power. What is needed is wisdom and the will to care and reverence.

Advent and Christmas are times of ultimate mystery. We are called to celebrate the mystery of God's love revealed in the Child Jesus. The mystery of God's love reaches unbounded proportions when we realize that Jesus is God's love revealed in a total, absolute and unconditional way. Jesus is God's absolute, never-to-be-taken-back Word of acceptance and salvation. In the mystery of this love, in this child, in this history, God redeems our human condition and offers us the hope of eternal life. The enemies of humankind, sin and death, will not have the final word in God's creation. The coming of God's Word is final and not to be defeated. This final, unconditional Word is LOVE.

This holy season and holy night speak to our hearts of the need to accept our acceptance. In Jesus, we are unconditionally and absolutely loved and accepted by the Father. The feelings of guilt, inferiority, hostility and hatred need not hold sway in our hearts. Through Jesus, we have been liberated from the darkness of such negative forces. We have been reborn with the birth of this Child. We can now walk in the light of a new day with Him who is Light and Life. The gift of this season and that holy night is the gift of God's healing Word. In the midst of our confusions, disappointments, defeats, sins, routines and hopes comes the Word which proclaims, "Peace on earth and good will to all who make room for this Child. Know that this night is not the night of darkness and the forces of evil. Rather, this night is holy and will break into the new dawn of the Light that will not be overcome. Into the anxieties that fill your heart, let Him who calms every fear speak His word of unconditional love. Above all, be still and listen in holy silence to the Word that makes all words meaningful. Come to the mystery of this night with a childlike faith in this Child born to each of us."

The unbounded love of God, revealed in Jesus, also speaks to us of our hope of glory. We not only pray that Jesus will be born into our hearts, but we hope that he will come again and find us ready. The Word has become flesh, and has made his dwelling within us. We not only look back in time to that first Holy Night, but we look forward to that day when the Lord will return in glory. Each time we celebrate the Eucharist, the Sacrament of Jesus Christ's love, we long for that day when "Christ will come again." Each time we remember the Lord, we proclaim his birth, death, resurrection and coming again in glory. We need not fear his return. The birth of Jesus speaks to us of the mystery of the God who so loved the world that He sent His Son to heal and redeem our brokenness. When he comes in the fullness of his glory, this love will be perfected in us. The day of the Lord will be one of Light and Life.

For now, we are caught in that uncomfortable position of sitting on the horn of a dilemma. There is no cushion of ease to which we can retreat, in the hope of living a comfortable life. To be a Christian is to know that inner tension of the "here and not yet." Through the indwelling of the Paraclete, Jesus is with us. Yet we know that sin and darkness continue to exercise influence in our lives. So we live, struggle and above all, hope for that day when the Lord Jesus will return to call us into the peace of his Kingdom. We draw close to the crib in gratitude and awe. In our inmost being, we cry out, "Come Lord Jesus! Come Lord Jesus!"